SACRAMENT OF PEACE

A Family Program to Help Children Celebrate Joyfully the Sacrament of Penance

CHiLDREN ASK QUESTiONS OF LiFE...
THE STEADFAST LOVE OF THEiR PARENTS WiLL HELP THEM TO DiSCOVER THEiR OWN ANSWERS SLOWLY AND PROGRESSiVELY.

PAULIST PRESS
NEW YORK/TORONTO

by
**FRANCOISE DARCY BERUBE
JOHN PAUL BERUBE**

An Unusual Book...

This book is part of a family program on penance which includes:

- a pastoral guide for priests and coordinators
- a booklet for children 7 to 8 years old
- a booklet for children 9 to 12 years old.

This book is not meant to be used only on one occasion, that of the child's first confession. You can refer to it over the years and find inspiration and practical suggestions concerning:

- the christian education of your children;
- the formation of their conscience;
- the preparation for their first confession;
- the customary celebration of the sacrament of penance for all the family;
- the deepening of prayer life in the home, etc.

The same thing applies to the children's booklet. It can be referred to not only for first confession but also

- for the preparation of future confessions;
- for prayer and reflection at any time.

All rights reserved.

Printed and bound in the United States of America

Copyright © 1974 by The Missionary Society of Saint Paul the Apostle in the State of New York

Table of Contents

Here is what you will find in your guide: Some guidelines on how to use your book

Part I:
The awakening and formation of christian conscience, from early childhood to the threshold of adolescence

- The psychological and moral development of the child — p. 7
- The pedagogy of a child's moral development — p. 13
- Formation of a christian conscience or gradual integration of moral development into the child's relationship with God. — p. 19
- The particular importance of experiencing reconciliation — p. 29

Part II:
The meaning of the sacrament of penance for us and for our children

- Doctrinal reflections on penance — p. 37
- At what moment should a child receive the sacrament of penance for the first time? — p. 46
- Long-term preparation for the sacrament of penance — p. 50

Part III:
A program preparing children of 7 to 8 years old for penance

- God who gives you life calls you to grow — p. 61
- God who is love calls you to love — p. 66
- God our Father invites you to love him, to pray to him — p. 73
- God our Father always forgives us — p. 76
- The Church invites us to celebrate together God's forgiveness — p. 84

Part IV:
A program preparing children of 9 to 12 years old for penance

- Look at the Lord and see how he loves you — p. 101
- Who are you? — p. 109
- Listen to God's call — p. 115
- How do you answer God's call? — p. 123
- God always forgives us — p. 129
- The Church invites us to celebrate God's forgiveness — p. 139

Part V:
Suggestions for family prayer life

- Family rites linked to mealtime — p. 148
- Family rites linked to evening prayer — p. 150
- Family discussions and celebrations — p. 151

Appendix:
In brief: 10 questions that bother parents — p. 155

How to Use Your Book?

Remark:
What we are suggesting is obviously not the only way to follow, nor the best way for everyone. This is simply some practical advice which will make the use of this book easier and more fruitful.

- Begin by leafing through the child's booklet in order to get an idea of its spirit and of its different parts.

    (Remember that there are two children's booklets, one for 7-8 year olds, and the other for 9-12 year olds. These are two very different books, designed to meet the needs of each age group.)

    The booklet should not be given to the child before the beginning of the program.

- Leaf through the third or the fourth part of your guide (depending on the age of your child) so that you realize the manner in which the program is set up.

- If you have time (if, for example, you are not planning on beginning the program for several months) you would find it very profitable to look through the first part of your guide "The awakening and formation of a christian conscience..." immediately. This will help you to understand better and to guide better the moral growth of your children regardless of age.

    This part, because much is being said in only a few pages, will perhaps seem a little difficult to you in certain places... Don't worry about it: everything will become clearer little by little as the program unfolds. Besides, the guide for priests and coordinators foresees a parent meeting dealing precisely with the question of the child's moral formation.

- Then quietly read the second part. This will allow you

    - to personally reflect on the sacrament of penance;
    - to better understand the current discussion concerning the age for confession;
    - to better see how to help your child in his day-to-day life during the months preceding the beginning of the program.

- Now you can familiarize yourself more with the actual program (see parts 3 or 4 of your guide).

    Each program is divided into stages. There are five stages for the 7-8 year olds, and six stages for the 9-12 year olds.

Study in depth one stage at a time, always using the child's booklet and your guide together. The better you understand the program, the better you can, when the time comes, adapt it to your child, your temperament and your family life style.

- The fifth part of your guide "Suggestions for the prayer life of the family" will probably interest you more towards the end of the program, but you should, of course, feel free to look at it whenever you wish.

N.B. In case some of our readers are disturbed about our use of exclusively masculine pronouns, we wish to say that in referring to "the child", we mean both sons and daughters. But as it would be awkward to keep writing (and reading) on every page the alternatives "she/he", "himself/herself", "her/him", we think that parents who are helping a daughter (or several children at once) to prepare for the celebration of penance will be quite willing to substitute the appropriate pronouns and adjectives in each case.

PART ONE

Psychological and Pedagogical Foundations of the Program

I. Psychological and Moral Development of the Child

An awakening of moral conscience does not suddenly manifest itself at the age of reason. This awakening is slow and progressive: it is linked to the general growth of the child, to his emotional, intellectual and social development.

For this reason, we will briefly describe several aspects of the general development of a child before beginning any discussion concerning the awakening of moral judgment.

1. A Brief Description of a Child's General Development

The principal stages in the harmonious development of a child's personality can be summarized in four charts.

Each of these charts will indicate three things:
- the basic experience necessary for a child;
- attitudes which can be awakened in him as a result of these experiences;
- attitudes educators should have in order to encourage his development.

Note:
The ages indicated are approximate ones only and depend greatly on each child's temperament and the quality of education he receives from his family environment.

The joy of being loved makes us capable of loving.

STAGE ONE: FROM 0 TO 2 YEARS

The child's experiences	Attitudes to be awakened in the child	Attitudes to be encouraged in the educator
• The experience of being fed, cared for, and loved • The experience of a stable love	• A basic confidence — in others — in himself — in life • A basically positive attitude: because he is loved, he feels worthy of that love	• Genuine, steadfast love • A relaxed and attentive presence

STAGE TWO: 2 TO 6 YEARS

The child's experiences	Attitudes to be awakened in the child	Attitudes to be encouraged in the educator

• The experience of
— having to grow, to progress
— being encouraged to take a chance
— being capable of
  • saying "no"
  • exercising self-control
  • making a choice
  • discovering better his sexual identity
 	
• The experience of meeting
— limits to his freedom
— an authority to be respected
	• A strengthening of self-awareness and self-confidence
	
	• A pride
	— in being able to say "no"
	— in being able to exercise self-control
	— in being able to choose
	— in being able to identify with the parent of the same sex
	
	• An ability to recognize his mistakes or his faults without losing his own self-respect
	
	• A capacity to accept limitations to his freedom imposed by authority or freedom of others
		• Respect for the initiatives of the child
		
		• Healthy attitude towards sexuality in general
		
		• Encouraging the child's identification with the parent of the same sex
		
		• Confidence in the child's abilities
		
		• A firm and loving control
		— which stimulates the child, urges him on, encourages him to progress, to use his freedom
		— which lets him become aware of his mistakes or faults without feeling humiliated
		— which helps him to accept and integrate the frustrations of his limitations

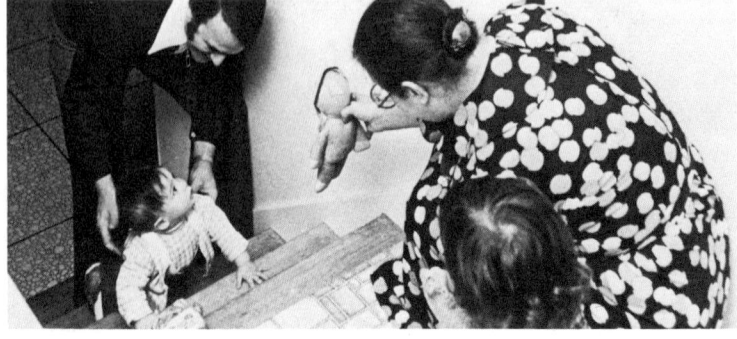

STAGE THREE: FROM 6 TO 9 YEARS

The child's experiences

The experience of	Attitudes to be awakened in the child	Attitudes to be encouraged in the educator

• having personal talents
• being able to succeed
• being able to discover different talents in others
• being able to count on help from others
• being able to help them
	• Accepting himself as a person with both talents and limitations
	• Desiring to develop his talents
	• Feeling confident that he can do this
	• Accepting others and their talents
	• Being able to ask for, or to give help, without making a big show of it
		• Recognition of a child's special talents
		• A true acceptance of the child's limitations
		• Confidence in the child
		  — which spurs him on to steady progress
		  — which helps him accept and then surmount his failures
		  — which rejoices with him in his successes

• being able to accept little responsibilities and to face the consequences of his actions	• Having a sense of joy for responsibilities suited to his age	— which helps him to face up to certain responsibilities

Note:
The key words to a child's development during these three stages are "growth and progress".

These words should express:
• a desire • an ability • an experience

For the child, the goals of these early stages can be summed up as follows:
- "You too can progress."
- "You are urged to progress."
- "You will be happy when you make progress."
- "You will make us happy by progressing."

STAGE FOUR: FROM 9 TO 12 YEARS
Following these stages, the child then reaches the pre-teen or latency period.

The child's experiences	Attitudes to be awakened in the child	Attitudes to be encouraged in the educator
• A growing awareness of his individual freedom, and of his responsibility for his own actions • A more conscious awareness of the demands, the difficulties and the joys of living together in a group	• A desire to play a part in the groups to which he belongs • A feeling of confidence that he can do this	• Accepting the growing importance which his peer group has for the child • Helping the child experience fully the social values which he has discovered, and helping him to live up to his responsibilities • Encouraging him at the same time to keep and to develop his own ideas and preferences
• An awareness of the role we can play in the different groups to which we belong	• An interest in and enthusiasm for group activities, for the value of belonging to a group: e.g. team spirit	• Creating opportunities for worthwhile group activities

Note:
— The key words concerning the development of the child in this fourth stage could be:
  • "becoming yourself"
  • "interacting with others."

— The educational goals could be summed up this way:
  • "You are capable of becoming yourself."
  • "You have a unique role to play."
  • "You need other people."
  • "Other people need you."

2. Development of Moral Judgment

Parallel to the general development of the child's personality, is the development of his moral judgment.

Two psychologists in particular have studied this question:
- PIAGET, some thirty years ago in Europe;
- KOHLBERG, in the past fifteen years in the U.S.A.

Briefly, here are their conclusions:

A. Development of moral judgment according to Piaget

According to Piaget, childhood is the time of a legalistic morality. Let us look at the principal characteristics of this morality:

a) *Up to the age of 8, any moral judgment the child may have is controlled by do's and don'ts.*

The things which are permitted and which are therefore good, are things which please grown ups.

The things which are forbidden and are therefore bad, are the things which displease them.

Children's actions are judged according to material results: e.g. breaking 10 plates without meaning to is more serious than breaking one plate angrily on purpose.

The motive behind many actions thus becomes fear of punishment or anticipation of a reward.

A child therefore does not really have any personal conscience. He has made the wishes of his parents a part of himself. We can say he has his parents inside of him! Psychology calls it the superego. At this age, the voice of his conscience is little more than the demands and orders of his parents.

b) *From the age of 8-9 and up to the age of 12-13*

Under the influence of his social experience, a child's moral judgment changes little by little.

What is considered to be good, becomes that which lets him live in harmony with other people.

Something is bad when it destroys friendship and confidence. For example, lying is a bad thing to do, not any longer because it is forbidden, but because it destroys confidence.

This is the age at which Law is seen as ensuring social order.

c) *From age 13 on*

The age of adolescence with its new ability to think abstractly, will gradually let the young person create an autonomous morality based on freely chosen values.

B. *Development of moral judgment according to Kohlberg*

The development sequence proposed by Piaget fits well into the more general and expanded description laid out by Lawrence Kohlberg, a psychology professor at Harvard University. According to Kohlberg, the basic criteria of moral judgment are divided into three levels of moral development.

Gradual Moral Judgment Development According to Kohlberg and Piaget

Level of morality	Criteria of moral judgment according to Kohlberg	Characteristics of Piaget's morality code
Pre-moral level		Heteronomy and Exteriority: first reference to exterior and authoritative norms
stage 1	I act or refrain from acting through fear of punishment.	
stage 2	I act to receive a reward.	
Level of conformist morality		
stage 3	I act to obtain social approval.	
stage 4	I act in order to respect the law and the order.	
Level of interiorised and personal morality		Autonomy and Interiority
stage 5	I act in order to respect others.	First references to values assumed by conscience
stage 6	I act in reference to general principles of goodness and social justice because I have personally assumed them.	

As we can see, both theories involve a movement from laws imposed by some outside force, towards values freely chosen by the individual.

It should be noted that Kohlberg's studies show that fewer than 33% of adult Americans ever reach stage 5. Some of those who reach stages 5 or 6 in their family relations, never progress beyond stages 1 or 2 in the areas of professional honesty, or vice versa.

II. Pedagogy of the Moral Development of the Child

General perspectives:
— To foster the progress of the child in moral reasoning we may mention two main ways:

- reflection on his life experiences, specially his social relationships;

- discussion of situations involving new and different values which can help him to pass from one stage of moral development to another one.

The main tool in this progress is dialogue (we will speak later about this).

— We also feel that the type of atmosphere in which the child is educated will greatly influence the maturation of his moral judgment. Indeed experience seems to prove that the more we surround the child with an authoritative system which eliminates his choices and risks, the more we retard his moral development.

On the contrary, the more we let the child makes choices in his moral life and help him reflect on their consequences, the more his liberty comes into play, (with risks and errors) and the greater is his progress towards maturity and moral judgment.

— However, as christian educators, we are concerned not only with maturity of moral judgment but equally with:

- the child's behavioral progress and thus his capacity to decisively choose what is good;

- the gradual integration of the child's moral life with his spiritual life, his relationship with God.

— From this double concern, come the two divisions of this chapter:

- pedagogical perspectives concerning the moral development of the young child;

- formation of a christian conscience or gradual integration of the child's moral development with his relationship to God.

1. Pedagogical Perspectives in the Moral Development of the Young Child

A. A negative principle

God should not be made a factor in the pre-moral or early moral formation of a child.

Why? Because there is a way of using God which can retard the development of the child's moral conscience and which can distort his view of God for a long time.

While the child is still completely under the influence of
- the "permitted" and the "forbidden"
- punishment and reward type of morality,

a close association of God with morality will result in his being considered:
- a policeman God
- a watchman God
- a God who punishes and rewards us here-and-now by means of our parents.

God becomes someone who reinforces the "superego", who imprisons the child in his childhood morality. This kind of God conforms only too well to the animistic tendencies in a child who believes in a mysterious justice that is constantly ready to punish him for his wrong-doings.

Obviously, in his early years, a child does need a precise code of what is permitted and what is forbidden, and a strong enough superego to let him learn little by little to control himself, to keep out of trouble and to live in our society. This stage however is one of pre-moral development dealing with training or conditioning but not with moral education as such.

Moral education as such should build on these first experiences, not in order to keep the child at this level, but rather to help him move out of it and gradually discover his own values, learn about freedom through experience, and become aware of his personal responsibilities.

Let us point out that we do not minimize the importance of a firm authority in the family. On the contrary, insecurity in the child is often the result of a lack of authority. He must face limitations in order to grow; the experience of obstacles will slowly teach him to repress his desires to possess everything, always to be first and always to do as he pleases. The art of authority lies in how we apply this principle.

B. *A positive principle*

The moral education of a young child should be a positive moral initiation into fundamental human values.

Two basic experiences make such an education possible:

- experiencing a loving relationship;

- experiencing a special quality of joy as a discovery of values.

a) *Experiencing a loving relationship*

Well before he is able to discuss it, a child has a vague idea of the values which guide his parents' lives. Without his being aware of it, what is important for them becomes important for him.

If, for example, parents usually treat persons and things with respect, children will easily pick up the same trait.

Robert is three years old. His grandmother is nearly blind. The child has, as it were, absorbed the parents' attitude of respect like part of the air he breathes. When he visits grandma, he seems to put aside his natural exuberance to become a delicate, attentive guide to her. The attitude of respect acquired through projection of a daily lived respect by his parents spontaneously influences Robert's behavior.

b) *Experiencing a special quality of joy*

In his relations in life with others, the child will discover certain values by the joy which they bring him. Let us consider a couple of examples.

1st example:

Erin is a rather exuberant and demanding little girl. Her mother had some work to do and asked Erin to play quietly in the next room and not to bother her. Erin did as her mother wanted. From time to time she peeped in the door without saying anything: her mother would raise her eyes and smile at her . . . Erin sensed that she was making her mother happy. This in turn made her happy and peaceful. She was experiencing a new value: cooperation, an experience which gave her a feeling of growth.

None of this is known explicitly by the child. Rather it is felt intuitively on an emotional level: but what is experienced on the subconscious level is very important. It can be described like this:

It is worth the great effort involved in order to experience this kind of deep inner joy.

Erin had often experienced the very real pleasure of being mischievous and troublesome, but had also experienced the unpleasant results of her actions: her mother would become angry, punish Erin, who in turn, would become unhappy, annoyed and feel lonesome.

Today, as a result of her efforts, she had experienced another kind of joy which filled her with a sense of well-being. This experience could be a dynamic force in her life, helping her to move from the punishment-reward stage to the social approval one.

2nd example:

A small, very intelligent boy, 7 years old, one day expressed his own view of this special kind of joy.

Johnny belonged to a family that was very poor and that didn't have candy very often. One day a neighbour took him to the fair and gave him some spending money. Later that afternoon she noticed that Johnny seemed to have something precious in his tightly closed hand. She asked him what he was hiding. He smiled and half opened his hand as if he was showing her a treasure: several sticky candies were visible!

— "Why don't you eat them?" the neighbour asked.
— "I'm saving them for Teddy (his four year old brother). He loves candy!"
— "But wouldn't you like to eat them yourself?"
— "Well yes . . . if I were to eat them I'd feel good here (pointing to his stomach) but when Teddy eats them I'll feel good here (pointing to his heart)!"

Don't these very simple but amazing words show the marvelous capacity of children to differentiate between the kinds of joy possible, and to choose freely among them?

Thus, little by little in the course of several years, a child will discover a variety of human values through the positive and negative experiences he has had.

C. Importance of dialogue about moral questions

As he grows older, he will be confronted by more complex situations, involving several values at once. He will find himself, as Kohlberg says, in a "cognitive-conflict situation" which can be for him an opportunity for progress.

It is here that the famous pedagogical tool known as dialogue should come into the picture:

- an affectionate, peaceful dialogue which does not try to impose values but which helps a child become more precisely aware of them as a result of his experience;

- a patient dialogue which will help the child to think, to progress at his own pace according to his developing convictions;

- a dialogue which teaches him, little by little, to know why he makes a certain choice and then to judge if the choice should be confirmed or modified.

It should be noted that we feel, as do several other educators, that the theories of the psychologists which show the young child as completely dominated by a legalistic morality could be misleading. We suggest it is a little more complex than this. Who can say that this stage in the child's development is not strengthened and prolonged by the very attitude adults have toward the child? Experience seems to show that in a favourable environment a child has a very precocious — even though occasional and fleeting — insight into values such as peace, cooperation, respect, generosity, courage, truth and justice.

D. A delicate problem: aggressiveness and instinctive reactions in the child

a) Aggressiveness

Aggressiveness is not a defect; it is a natural dynamism by which the child mobilizes his own powers to attain his aims.

The manifestations of aggressiveness are numerous and vary according to many factors: age, sex, education and environment.

Aggressive tendencies are part of normal child development. To prevent their expression or ignore such manifestations can injure a normal child's development or provoke psychic trauma.

But the aggressive behavior of the child both provokes and disturbs us. So we are tempted to stop it quickly and reproach the child, thus making him feel very guilty. Even if he seems to calm down nothing is really solved. The child is frustrated, represses his aggressive feelings before us, but expresses them behind our back. No proper education takes place in this manner.

Education takes place when the child learns to dominate his aggressivity and to direct it constructively.

Some practical advice can be useful here:

- Tolerate the child's verbal expressions directed at us or others, as well as some physical aggressiveness.

- Stop immediately, however, aggressive manifestations that could be harmful to himself or others.

- Later on, when the child is calm, show him that you understand his moments of aggressiveness, as you sometimes experience them too.

  The child often fears his aggressiveness and needs reassurance.

- Teach him the importance of control. Take advantage of the least occasion to let him experience the joy and pride of any progress in this field as in others.

- Help him discover that this energy within him can be a tremendous force to enable him to succeed in many activities and projects.

Treat moments of anger as "difficult moments" rather than sins.

We all know that young children often have fits of anger, at times violent and sudden. Let us avoid associating anger with sin. Let us treat it as a difficult situation, much as we would treat a "storm", something we wish to protect ourselves and others against. However, when all is calm again, let us dialogue with the child. Starting with his experiences, we will help him see the danger of anger which leads us to do things we deeply regret afterwards.

This is why it is important for us: • to learn step by step to conquer anger,

• and thus to take means to do so.

b) *Instinctive reactions*

One must avoid associating the idea of sin with the instinctive reactions where the child's liberty cannot be involved.

In this field must be placed spontaneous behavior inspired by fear, insecurity, the desire to be chosen, preferred, the desire to be first, etc., in other words all that is linked to the spontaneous egocentrism of the child and to his violent reactions whenever he feels frustrated.

Sin should not be spoken of before the child is around 7 years old and should then only be linked with conscious and deliberate choices. The following pages will explain this in greater detail.

III. Formation of a Christian Conscience or Gradual Integration of Moral Development into the Child's Relationship with God.

1. Moral Experience and Religious Experience

If we should not make God a part of the moral formation of a young child, the following question can be raised:

What difference is there between a non-christian child and a christian child when both have been morally well educated?

By definition the difference cannot be found to be a difference in values nor in degrees of perfection. Little by little the difference will be seen at the level of spiritual experience, where morality will gradually become internalized in the child and will become an integral part of his relationship with God, a way of entering into God's Plan.

Let's take a child who, at the same time as he is forming a genuine human morality, gradually discovers God through the faith of his parents, and comes to recognize the love of God in his everyday life. What will happen to him?

Bit by bit, with patient help from us, this child will link the two aspects of his experience, and his moral life will become also a religious experience, taking on a new and deeper meaning.

An example will explain better what we mean.

Mark	Luke
1. He has already experienced the joy of pleasing and serving others even at the price of a difficult effort	1. He also has already experienced the joy of loving others.
2.	2. One day Luke finds out that by loving others, he also pleases God.
3. At times he feels in his heart a call to love this way. (It is God's call but the child doesn't know it.)	3. In the call felt in his conscience he recognizes now the call of God.
4. He experiences an inner happiness when he answers that call. (It is the joy of God's presence but he doesn't know it.)	4. He feels this same joy, but lives it also in praising God because he knows that God's Spirit is with him to help him love others.
Moral experience is not conscious of its religious dimension.	Moral experience gradually becomes christian experience as it integrates itself into a relationship with God.

Let us make this more explicit in several simple statements:

In the call to certain values which he has already experienced, the christian child will become aware of a call from God.

- His free response becomes a personal answer to the love of God.

- He gradually learns to make the joy he feels in doing the right thing, a part of the humility and thanksgiving he feels toward God who is the source of all good.

- We might say that his relationship with other people will be considered as part of his relationship with God.

- His moral wrong-doing will be recognized as a refusal to answer God's call.

- His remorse will take the form of repentance and asking for God's forgiveness.

- His efforts in the area of morality will be coupled with an increasing reliance on God's strength.

- Reconciliation with another person will be seen also as reconciliation with God.

What is true for a child is equally true for an adult. The difference between two men, one Christian and the other non-Christian, both of whom are trying to live and serve the same values (and this is becoming more and more common these days), is not found at the level of moral qualities, which may be identical. The difference is this: for the Christian, living these values becomes also a religious experience, an answer to God's call, an entry into his plan of salvation.

The basic pedagogical question which is then raised is:

When and how should the child be encouraged gradually to integrate his moral life with his religious life, i.e. with his prayer life and his relationship to God?

Dynamic Development of the Moral Experience and the Religious Experience

From 2 to 6 years old

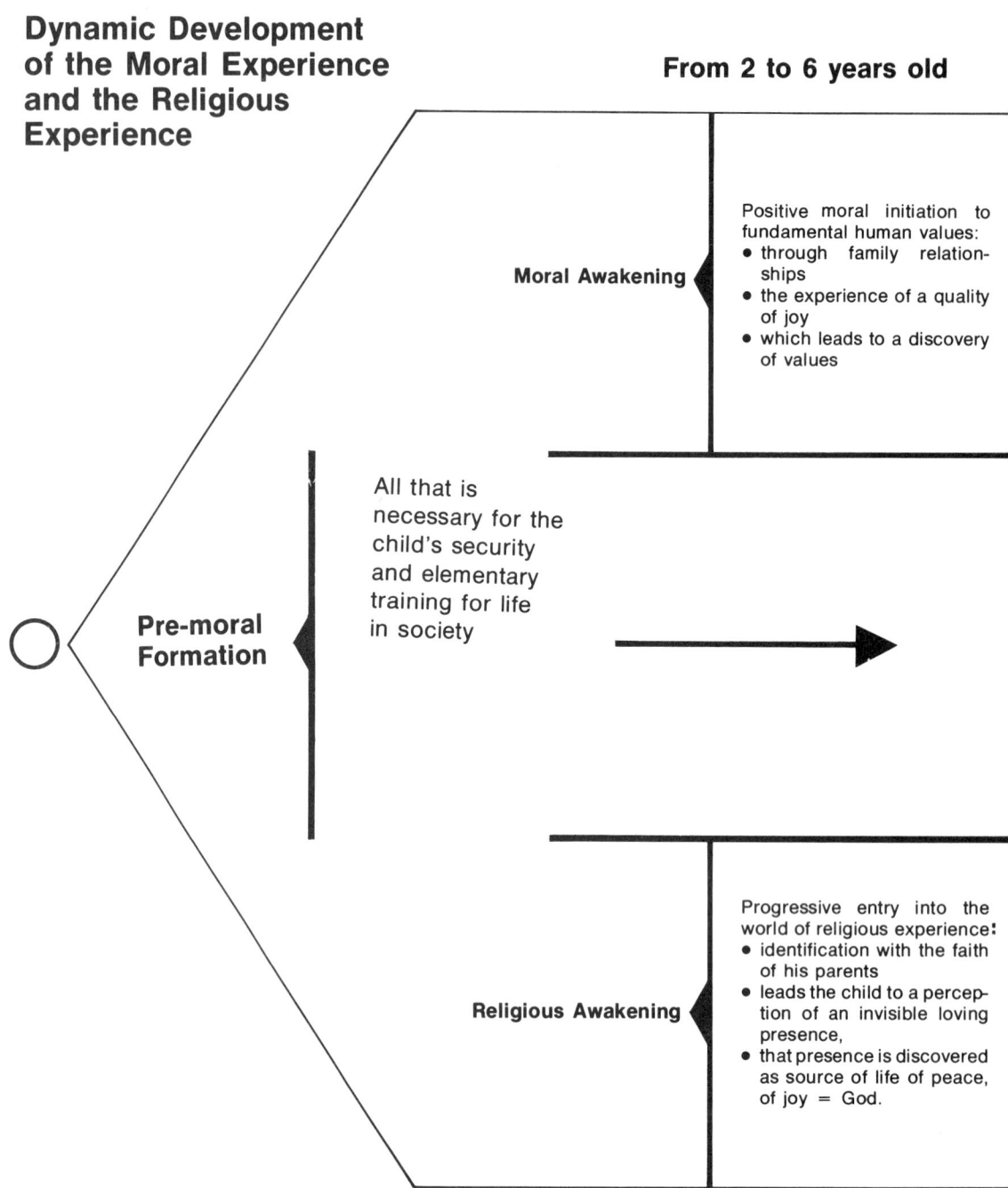

Pre-moral Formation: All that is necessary for the child's security and elementary training for life in society

Moral Awakening: Positive moral initiation to fundamental human values:
- through family relationships
- the experience of a quality of joy
- which leads to a discovery of values

Religious Awakening: Progressive entry into the world of religious experience:
- identification with the faith of his parents
- leads the child to a perception of an invisible loving presence,
- that presence is discovered as source of life of peace, of joy = God.

Family Community

From 6 years old and on...

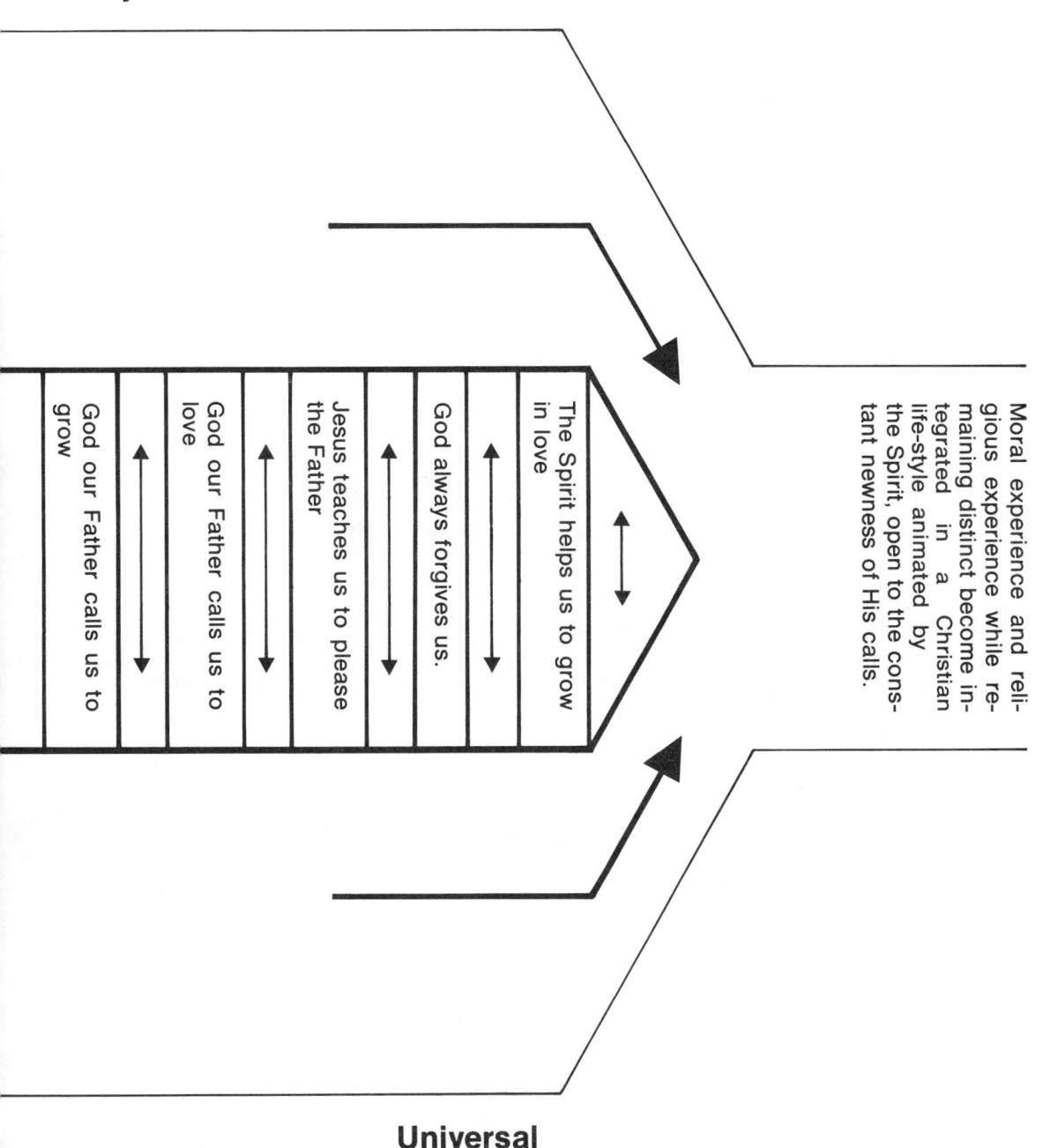

+ **Local Christian Community** + **Universal Christian Community**

2. Stages Involved in Integrating These Two Types of Experiences

Several stages can be distinguished in the dynamics or general movements of this process (see Chart, p. 22).

Stage 1: *Without linking the two, encourage the parallel development of a religious awakening and a moral awakening.*

As previously mentioned, a moral awakening occurs:

- in the threads of human development,
- by experiencing a certain kind of happiness,
- which leads to the discovery of values.

In the same way, the first stirrings of a religious awakening are fostered by:

- the child's relationship with his parents,
- his coming in contact with certain parental attitudes
  — which raise questions in his mind
  — and lead to the discovery of a presence known as God.

This religious awakening can briefly be described in more detail.

— Discovering God's name and presence

- Noticing his parents becoming recollected and talking to someone whom he can't see ... will raise a question in even a small child's mind.
- He will learn of a name, a name which his parents say with respect, joy, a special love: God, Our Father, Lord ...
- He will hear this name again from time to time during moments of wonder, joy, intense living, love ...
- Over a period of time this name will become for him a "Presence". It will be a mysterious presence which will be associated with some of the best aspects of his existence: life, love, joy, wonder.

— Beginning to pray with his parents

- Gradually, after having seen and heard his parents praying — he will join in with them not only by respecting the "minute of silence" before praying, or by his gestures but also by a few words of prayer which he can say with his parents. These should be words of joy, thanksgiving, love, confidence in the love of God, who gives him life, a beautiful world, and who brings us together in love and peace.

Thus in his own way, a child has entered in the world of religious experience through emotional identification with the faith of his parents. The invisible God with whom he can communicate by an occasional prayer has become a part of his life.

It is mainly God the Father who should be mentioned to the very young child. Jesus can also be mentioned occasionally, not as a model for behavior, but as the Son of God, who came to tell us about the marvelous God that we would like to know more about.

Stage 2: *Begin building bridges between the religious and the moral experiences of the child.*

This stage could begin at about the age of six and could be continued when the child enters a more formal religious education program.

But it should be emphasized that the religious formation of children in Grade One should be basically oriented towards the sense of wonder involved in a discovery of the mystery of God, of his loving presence. Any focus on morality should be slight, infrequent and positive.

Here are some suggestions for building the bridges:

a) *God urges us to grow*

> A child is aware of the fulfilment he feels and the happiness he brings his parents when he progresses in any areas of his life.
> Sometimes,
> - the joy of God our Father can be mentioned as echoing his own and that of his parents;
>
> - God's desire that we make the effort necessary to grow can be mentioned.
>
> Little by little an assertion, seen as a call motivated by love, becomes obvious:
>
> Because God loves us,
> he wants us to grow,
> to become more and more fully alive
> and to make progress in all areas.

b) *God calls us to love*

> Through his experience, a child will discover the peace of cooperation and the joy of loving.
>
> Here again, when a child acts in a loving way, he should be told of God's joy and his desire to see us, his children, united in love.

Gradually another idea will be offered as an invitation:

"God's joy is to love.
He invites us to share in his joy by living together in love."

This would be the right time to present Jesus as someone who brings God great joy, and who came to teach us how to make God happy too.

The following could be introduced at that time:

- several of the Gospel accounts which show Jesus' great love for all men;

- some of the words of Jesus which urge us to love one another.

Stage 3: *Help the child use his negative experiences to deepen his relationship with God.*

As he progressively becomes more conscious that the call of God reinforces the appeal of values which are already present in his life, a child will gradually become aware that when he refuses a call to these values, he is also refusing the call of God.

This is a very delicate and important moment in his christian development. A lack of tact or perception could distort his image of God.

Let us try to see the various facets of the problem, first of all concerning the experience of the child, secondly, the steps we should help him take, and thirdly, the educational attitudes which are best suited to the problem.

a) *The experience of the child*

What happens in the child's experience?

- He becomes more aware of his limitations, and his faults: "It's hard to love like God asks us, to make an effort to grow — sometimes I don't want to . . . "

- His feelings of guilt become greater because he begins to feel guilty before God.

- He runs the risk of feeling deeply crushed and discouraged by his faults and his moral failings.

b) *The steps we must help him take to overcome these difficulties*

These can be described as follows:

- Agree with his new awareness:

    "It's true that when I refuse to grow or to love, I am rejecting God's call, I am not making him happy, I am a sinner."

- Try to arouse a feeling of confidence:
  — "God still loves me, he always forgives me".
  — "He is with me so that he can help me to progress. He is counting on me."

- Help him discover that in the joy of forgiveness and human reconciliation, we also find the love and joy of the God of peace.

  (These experiences are of utmost importance; a special paragraph on page 32 will be devoted to this.)

c) *Three pedagogical attitudes the child needs to find in us*

- Help the child to understand that we are sharing his experience: we are not innocent judges condemning a wrongdoer. We are all sinners, all needing forgiveness, all trying to "learn how to love".

- Make the child feel that he still has all our love, all our esteem, all our confidence.

  In order to do this, absolutely everything that could destroy his opinion of himself by teaching him to identify too closely with his faults, should be avoided. Our attitudes should help the child say: "I did something very wrong, but I know I can do better." We should avoid everything that would make him think: "I am evil, and there is nothing I can do about it."

- Take as much time as is necessary to experience deeply with the child, the moments of forgiveness and reconciliation which occur in life.

  (As this is very important, there will be a special paragraph on it; see page 30).

Conclusion

These thoughts can be summed up by two important remarks:

— Basically christian morality is a human moral experience which is gradually integrated into a religious experience, and which as a result, takes on a new dimension and a new meaning.

— However, in the total experience of living a christian life there are two aspects which are specifically christian, and foreign to the non-religious moral experience.

- The first aspect concerns religious attitudes which, if this expression can be used, become moral obligations. They can be condensed into two main areas:

    the worship we should give God (or the call to glorify him);

    the apostolic responsibility (or the call to share the joy of the Good News).

    It can also be mentioned that the Gospel suggests emphasis on certain values such as the forgiveness of wrongdoings, patience during suffering, and a spirit of sacrifice. We strive for these values by imitating Christ and by participating in his plan of salvation.

- The second aspect is concerned with the means of moral progress. Because of his faith, a christian believes in the power of supernatural means to overcome evil in his life and in the world. These means are prayer and the sacraments, both privileged moments in his relationship with God.

IV. Particular Importance Attached to the Experience of Reconciliation

We can never have everything "in exact order" in christian morality. Why? Because christian morality is not a series of exact laws, rather it is a call to a never-ending growth in love: "Be perfect as your Heavenly Father is perfect" wrote Matthew (Mt. 5:48).

Which Luke took as meaning:
"Be merciful as your Heavenly Father is merciful" (Luke 6:36).

And which Jesus made even clearer:
"Love one another as I have loved you" (John 13:34).

Thus if christian morality is a constant call to progress, it is also a call to change, to transform ourselves.

Now psychology has stated that two conditions are necessary before such a change can take place. Carl Rogers wrote:
"Change appears to come about through experience in a relationship."

And again:
"We cannot change, we cannot move away from what we are until we thoroughly accept what we are."

In order that a child can gradually become capable of responding to the constant newness of God's call, he must first experience a significant relationship with us which will result in his being able to

- realistically accept himself,

- try to change, to be converted, to progress.

The experience of reconciliation, with its double form of receiving and giving forgiveness, is a fundamental experience in the course of this progress, of this call, mentioned above.

This theme can be developed in three points:

1. The child must be given a chance to experience in depth, moments of human reconciliation.

2. Little by little, he should be helped to discover in the joy of human forgiveness and reconciliation, the love and joy of the God of Peace.

3. And finally, when the time comes, he must be helped to see that the sacrament of penance is a liturgical celebration of a reconciliation with God and with others, which he has experienced in his everyday life.

1. A Child Must be Given a Chance to Experience in Depth, Moments of Human Reconciliation

A. Take time for forgiveness

When a child has done something seriously wrong, and when he comes to ask your forgiveness, don't answer in a rush as if it were not important. Take seriously this new response of the child.

- Take time to talk with him, to listen to him, to show him that your love has not changed.

- In this atmosphere, help him to become better aware of what he did wrong, to accept his difficulties, to accept himself.

- Draw his attention to the future, show him you are confident that he can do better, that he can change, and that you are there to help him.

- Take time to enjoy with him the peace of reconciliation by doing something together: either working or playing, or sharing something with him: candy or cookies.

B. Teach him to forgive also

When it is his turn to forgive someone, help him to do it wholeheartedly.

- Try to understand any hesitation, any problems on his part.

- Encourage him to make some sign of forgiveness to help the other person take the right steps.

- Give him a chance to discover the pure joy that comes to us when we try to forgive one another as God forgives us!

C. *Experience these moments of reconciliation as a family*

In every family there are days when everybody seems to be on edge, quarrelsome, gloomy or sulky.

When a way of reconciliation is found at last, try to bring it out, to celebrate it together in one way or another.

Example: It was the Martin family's first day of vacation. They arrived at their cottage at 2 p.m. It was raining, the house was dirty, and choosing bedrooms, dividing up the luggage and the chores to be done, led to all kinds of arguments and even scuffles. Both the parents and the children were on edge and angry.

When it was supper time, mother said that in no way could the family sit down to eat in that state of mind. She asked everyone to take a few minutes to calm down and then to come to dinner "with a smiling face"!

This was done. The meal, which was rather quiet in the beginning, gradually became more lively. When they had finished, the sun was shining, and father suggested everyone go for a walk together before doing dishes.

The walk and doing the dishes were completed with an air of enthusiasm . . . each person showing, without words . . . their joy in the reconciliation.

2. Help the Child to Discover Gradually that in the Joy of Reconciliation Is Found Also the Presence and Peace of God

A. The internal dynamism of the steps involved in reconciliation

As was previously stated, during the child's early years it is not advisable to mix moral formation and religious formation. But when he is about six years old, we can begin to build *bridges* between these two processes. We shall gradually lead the child to discover, in his daily experiences of reconciliation, God's presence, his call and his forgiveness.

The internal dynamism of the reconciliation process is the same for everyone. But the Christian experiences also in this process a redeeming encounter with God.

A diagram may help make this clearer:

The development of moral experience	**The religious experience that accompanies this development**
• I sense an uneasiness, an interior tension, a feeling of remorse.	• Because I live in God's presence, the remorse I feel becomes repentance.
• I realize that I have done wrong, I admit my faults	• I realize that in hurting my brother, I have sinned against God, I confess my faults to God.
• I feel a desire to correct this, and I decide what I should do.	• In my desire to correct this situation, I recognize the call of God, I open myself to his Spirit.
• I make some gesture of reconciliation and I am at peace again with myself and with others.	• Depending on God's strength, I make some gesture of reconciliation through which I am at peace again with myself, with others and with God.

B. The progressive discovery of God's presence at the very heart of the steps involved in reconciliation

Thus, we must very delicately, and very gradually, help the child to discover the call of God and His presence at the heart of his experiences. This can be done by using incidents in his daily life to express our faith in God to him.

For example: Some day when he is struggling to forgive someone, pray with him that the Holy Spirit will give him the courage to forgive.

Try to make him aware of God's joy in seeing his children reconciled.

— Sometime when he comes to ask your forgiveness, remind him of the loving presence of God who forgives him just as you do.

— When certain meaningful family incidents occur, like the one experienced by the Martin family mentioned above, it would be good if the parents put into words for everyone, the religious dimension of the experience.

Thus on the evening of that first day of vacation, the father invited the whole family to share together in a few moments of prayer. He called to mind the joy God feels when he sees His children reunited in peace. He recalled Jesus' invitation to us to love one another, to forgive each other. Together everyone prayed to the Holy Spirit to help them be more attentive to this call.

3. The Progressive Discovery of the Links Between These Experiences of Reconciliation and the Sacrament of Penance

Later on, when the child reaches the age for receiving the sacrament of penance, care should be taken that he grasps the link between the sacrament and his everyday life.

Like other sacraments, penance should be experienced, before being celebrated:

- If worship and brotherly love have no place in ordinary life, then participation in the Eucharist becomes nothing more than an empty ritual, devoid of meaning.

- The sacrament of christian marriage consecrates a very real love, which already exists, and which will be helped to grow in the image of Christ's and the Church's love. If there is no love there, one may well wonder what meaning the sacrament of marriage can have.

- If the steps involved in penance and reconciliation have no place in our lives, then the sacrament is nothing more than a magical rite without any real connection with our existence.

The sacrament of penance should be presented to the child
— not so much as something necessary before he can be forgiven,
— but as an invitation to celebrate with the rest of the christian community, the forgiveness which God gives us in our daily lives.

It is important to view it, not as an obligation, but rather as a priviledge: a special encounter with God that strengthens our courage and joy.

Don't leave the child with the impression that the sacrament is just the act of confession; show him as well the importance of other elements in the celebration:
- we pray to God;
- we acknowledge that we are sinners;
- we ask God's forgiveness;
- we praise him because he always forgives us;
- we pray to the Holy Spirit that we will grow in love;
- and we leave feeling stronger and happier, more united with Jesus and with others.

Later, depending on the time when the child becomes to some extent capable of serious and deliberate wrongdoings as he nears adolescence, we can insist more on the aspect of obligation.

It should be noted that to the extent that our celebrations of penance are really meaningful, innovative and satisfying for us and for our children, they will willingly come to them... If it takes a lot of coaxing to make them come, it means that they find them boring. The answer doesn't lie in reinforcing the obligatory aspect, but rather in making the celebrations more meaningful!

PART TWO

The Meaning of the Sacrament of Penance for Us and for our Children

SECTION ONE
Doctrinal Reflections on Penance

I. A Sacrament to Rediscover

1. The Crisis of Penance

The crisis of the sacrament of penance is now evident: the line-up at the confessional doors has diminished and the time between confessions has lengthened!

Why this situation? Some blame it on the "easy life" of Christians, a weakening of faith and of the meaning of sin, and the changes in the Church since Vatican II. Others direct their attacks to the outmoded liturgy of the sacrament of penance, with its exaggerated emphasis on individual and on secondary aspects of the christian life. Who is right? Probably every one, in varied degrees, has some truth in his favor.

2. The Crisis Is Not New

The sacrament of penance is not in its first crisis! Awareness of this saves us from overdramatizing the present situation. There were times in the Church's history when Christians scarcely went to confession at all and when it was necessary to profoundly change the sacrament in order to renew it.

A crisis is not necessarily a sign of decay. It is often a manifestation of vitality and growth. All development has its price.

3. A Crisis Which Concerns Us

What can we do? The question is asked of each of us. We can't afford to simply sit back and wait for happy days again. The renewed vitality of the sacrament is not the problem of the clergy alone. It is a concern of the first order for us since we are the Church. We all should be working for the development of necessary reforms.

Among the things we can do, one is of fundamental importance: rediscover for ourselves the meaning of the sacrament of penance.

A true renewal starts from within us. We must believe in the value of penance, with our mind and heart, otherwise what sense would it make to celebrate the sacrament ourselves and to prepare our children for it?

4. Direction of Our Research

Strange as it may seem, we will not start with the rites of the sacrament for two reasons:

— First, the rites are often meaningless; a few gestures in an anonymous "black box" can hide the real significance of the sacrament.

— Second, the rites will have to change during the years ahead. We are suggesting a more solid starting point.

Let's begin with life itself. Before finding penance crystallized in a ceremony, we first find it in life itself. If a sacrament is no longer nourished by life, it risks withering like a tree cut off at its roots.

5. The Help of a Sound Guide

To speak of penance involves us in a difficult and confusing discussion. The word "penance" is a vehicle of many incomplete or false notions.

We need to base our discussion on a solid guide: the Gospel. Jesus began his preaching by speaking of penance: "The time has come, and the kingdom of God is close at hand. Repent, and believe the good news" (Mark 1, 15).

The meaning of the above call is:

"Repent, that is do not be content with just exterior practices. Change your way of thinking and living. Turn your heart and your entire self towards God."

Penance is not superficial; it is a movement which we experience deep within ourselves in the secret place where we make the fundamental options of our life.

It is important, therefore, to keep in mind this perspective throughout the following pages.

II. Penance at the Center of Our Life

Penance, as we have said, begins in life and then expresses itself in a rite. It is this experience of penance as a process that we are going to develop.

1. We Are Divided Beings

— When we compare who we are with who we wish to become, we discover a gap, a distance.

Example:
- We want harmony in our home but we often sow discord.

- Someone needs help but we delay giving it.

- We are capable of making valuable contributions to the life of the city, but we prefer keeping busy with our own affairs.

— This gap, this distance between our ideals and our actions can be more or less serious.

- There are mere "accidents" along the way which do not change the fundamental direction of our life.

Example:

I am usually honest in my professional work. I even refuse "glasses of wine" or "subtle bribes". But suddenly I give in under the pressure of a friend in a bad situation. I do not even weigh the consequences of my action.

- On the other hand, my conduct at times leads me to a dangerous alienation which reduces my freedom more and more — thus endangering my life project.

Example:

I am involved in an extramarital affair. My wife knows nothing about it, I try my best to play the game but basically I well know I am not truly being myself, neither with my wife, nor with the other person concerned. I am in a situation which seriously jeopardizes the future of my marriage.

— Thus to measure the seriousness of this gap, of this alienating experience I am living, it is important not to look at the act alone, but to ask myself what started me off in that direction. Let's use the example of a lie:

I lied to a person. Why? Maybe it was only because I was taken by surprise or perhaps it was because he had no business knowing. But it could be also because for quite awhile I tended to be untruthful in my relationships with others.

In the end, the accumulation of "failings" count less than the mark these failings leave on my life.

2. We Need Reconciliation

No one can live such a split level existence indefinitely. Instinctively everyone searches for ways to overcome this kind of uneasiness. Here are some examples.

A) I forget

Faced with my failures, I take flight! I try to forget my troubles... I let myself take on a flurry of activities: business, travel, meetings, leasure, etc.

In other words, I lose touch with myself.

B) I refuse

At one moment I readily face my faults, but in the next I put them out of sight like a bad memory. I put them aside and I try to recapture my conscience as if it were still "lily white"... briefly, I refuse to assume responsibility for my actions.

C) I resign myself

This attitude is more realistic because I recognize my faults as my own. But I look for subtle excuses and say to myself: "That's the way it is... What can one do?... Everyone does it." This is the typical reaction of a conformist or a fatalist.

D) I accept

In this last case, I clearly assume responsibility for my past actions. I acknowledge that I did them, even if they displease me. "Yes, that is indeed what I did."

This attitude, as we can see, is worthy of man. It also is the only one which permits a sincere reconciliation.

3. The Christian Lives Reconciliation in Reference to God

A) *What is sin?*

For Christians a fault takes on a deeper dimension. It is not only my own affair, but an affair which also concerns God. This is why the name "sin" is given to it in the Bible.

Here we are liable to ask ourselves in what way could God concern himself with our faults. It is clear that, in one sense, our actions are not able to hurt God because God is God, that is he who is the infinite above all.

Yet, we must affirm that our sins do concern God. Why? Because God's design for each of us is that we become united with him in love and liberty.

Each time we sin, therefore, we contradict God's design for us. We diminish love and liberty in ourselves as well as in others. We prevent ourselves from becoming what we could be. Briefly we make a breach in the extraordinary "love story" God wishes to live with us.

That is why sin is much more than transgressing a taboo; it is more than merely breaking a law, or usurping the rights of others. Sin is a drama. It is enough to look at the crucified Christ to become convinced of this.

In order to recognize this drama, my faith must be alive. God must be real and alive for me. Otherwise I can never understand sin for what it is.

B) *Sin and reconciliation*

The Christian seeking reconciliation turns towards God. He acknowledges his faults. For him sin is an infidelity to God's love. But at the same time he turns to this love that can recreate him. God alone can restore the work of God that has been impaired by man.

This is the reason why, with light and understanding, the Christian realizes that he cannot make a total judgment of himself. God has supreme judgment and he alone measures liberty and all the complexity of human situations.

A Christian knows he is a sinner. Moreover, he is convinced that he will always remain one. He is not hopeless because of this certainty. On the contrary, for him it is another reason for constant gratitude to God. The more we are aware of our state of sinners, the more we feel thankful to God who watches over us even though we are not worthy of his care.

This is why we overcome our guilt feelings and experience confidence and serenity. "Even if our heart condemns us, says John, God is greater than our heart" (I Jn 3, 20).

4. Reconciliation Demands Gestures and Actions

The above statements should not be conducive to easy living. God is not a permissive soft Father who closes his eyes on our escapades. On the contrary the Bible says that he is a jealous God, who strongly desires that we respond to his love.

To live a reconciliation means to put back in place the love we refused. That means actions and gestures.

Example: I see that God has become a poor relation in my life plan, the one to whom I only leave "crumbs"... I am sorry and I ask God's forgiveness. Is this sufficient for reconciliation? My "being sorry" even when sincere, may be verbal only. My sincerity must be put to the test. In other words at the very moments I decide to put God fully into my life, reconciliation becomes for me a reality. Jesus tells us: "It is not he who says 'Lord, Lord' who will enter the kingdom of heaven but he who does the will of my Father" (Mt 7, 21).

Another example: I got angry with X... Who is to blame? At first I felt it was he. But, with time, I recognize my share of the responsibility. We have not met since the incident and I don't try to establish contact. To myself I say: "Forget it, this is an old story." I still celebrate the Eucharist and receive communion without scruples. Am I really reconciled with God? No, because I am not yet reconciled with my brother. Let's listen to Jesus: "You then, if you are bringing your offering to the altar and there remember that your brother has something against you, leave your offering there before the altar, go and be reconciled with your brother first" (Mt 5, 23).

We are now at the very heart of the Gospel. God himself is hurt in a brother that we harm, whoever he may be: spouse, friend, work companion, etc. And our return to God can only be accomplished through the "living sacrament" of our reconciliation with our brother. It is impossible to be at peace with God as long as I refuse a gesture of friendship. I must show that I wish to repair the harm done to others.

5. God Is at the Heart of Our Gestures of Reconciliation

"Without me you can do nothing" (Jn 15, 5). This sentence is without loopholes. God is the one who makes us able to answer his call, to act as his children, to take steps towards reconciliation. "It is God who saves us, not our deeds" (Gal 2, 16).

The salvation given to us by God affects our daily lives. We sometimes imagine things in the following way: life is where we sin, sacraments where we are forgiven. This is entirely false. God's free gift of love is not "fenced in" by the rites of the Church's liturgy. God's love is in all phases of history. This is the meaning found in the Resurrection. The Spirit of Jesus acts in the heart of all men.

That is why each time we return to God we are, as John says, "passing from death to life", entering by the power of God himself the new world of the Resurrection.

III. The Sacrament, a "High Point" in the Experience of Penance

A) An Invitation to Celebrate

A question arises! Why a sacrament, when we know that reconciliation takes place during actual living? When we ask the above question we also ask "why the Church?" and even "why Christ?" Sacraments are primarily special signs through which Jesus gives us life in the Church.

All sacraments speak of Jesus and his work of salvation. Sacraments tell us that Jesus assures us of passing from death to life. Each sacrament does this in its own way. Baptism, for instance, places the emphasis on a new birth which comes to us from the Spirit through water. The Eucharist emphasizes the bread of life which unites us in the body of Christ. Penance stresses Jesus' welcome that constantly helps us to rise again.

When we grasp this, we understand that sacraments are not received but celebrated, just like birth, love, and freedom.

This occurs also for forgiveness. Let us remember what we felt when we had to forgive, not a stranger, but someone dear who had hurt us deeply. How many hesitations, doubts, and apprehensions we experienced! "It's to difficult, I can't stand it... something between us is dead forever... why begin all over again...?"

To begin again: yes, that's the point; to give back our love, our trust, to become vulnerable again... To begin again: not simply to erase it all, to act "as if" nothing had happened, but to start again at the breaking point, making of this failure an opportunity to come in touch with one another more deeply and to advance together towards the future.

How difficult is a true reconciliation! Is it not a kind of spiritual death that we experience when we face it? But when at last we finally "give in", what a resurrection!

Joy — that other name for life — is born anew between us! And how can we know where it is greater: in the one who forgives or in the one who is forgiven? So, shouldn't the Church celebrate the joy of God and the joy of man which is echoed in her very heart?

"There is great joy in heaven, says the Gospel, when a sinner returns to God and does penance" (Luke 15, 7). There is also great joy on earth when a Christian returns to God and to the christian community. This joy is worth celebrating — this moment that has great significance in everyone's life, when we are created again in love by God's own Spirit.

We can now better understand how our life and the sacrament are interrelated. When after a dispute we come back to someone, then we already are living the sacrament of penance, we have initiated the process of penance. And that is why the Church invites us to come together and to complete the process by celebrating in the christian community that reconciliation which began in our own life. The Church wants us to hear from her in the sacrament the words of peace that God is speaking to us in our life. Thus the deep unity of christian life and the sacraments is strongly emphasized.

B) A Parable to Reflect on

By means of a story Jesus teaches us how to consider the sacrament of penance. We already know his parable of the Prodigal Son. Perhaps we know it too well or too little. Is it not significant that we call this story that of the "Prodigal Son", even though the father is the main character in the story? By his faithful love, he is the one who brings about the return of his son. If the son had not been sure of this love, he would have been too discouraged ever to return.

When the "prodigal son" returns, what happens? Is there a long inquiry with excuses or reprimands? No, the son does not even have time to apologize. His father does not wait; he is beside himself with joy. "Quickly", he says, "bring your best garments... kill the fatted calf and let us celebrate, for my son who was dead lives again" (Luke 15, 11-25). Such is God's forgiveness. It is without measure, unconditional, and gratuitous. Unfortunately we often wrap up the sacrament in the severity of a tribunal where fear is a dominant trait. How far we have come from the joyful feast of the parable!

C) The Meaning of the Confession and Reparation

a- Confession of sins

If we look upon the confession of our sins as a careful "bookkeeping" operation or as a humiliation we must endure at all cost, then it is understandable that we find problems with it because we are still trapped by the tribunal perspective.

But if we look at the confession of our sins in the context of a celebration of reconciliation and hope, then it takes on a very different meaning. It becomes the expression of our desire to be true to ourselves and to the community:

• True to ourselves: when expressing our faults to the priest we take off our masks and face ourselves as we are. Thus we can realize better the greatness of God's love reaching out for us in the depth of our sinfulness.

• True to the community: similarly the conversation carried on with the priest who represents the community places us in a relationship with it. We realize more clearly what it can expect of us and how our conduct hinders or harms its welfare.

b- Reparation or penance

The same reasoning holds true for the "penance" given to us by the priest. It is not a punishment for our sins but it is an invitation to show God and our brothers where we intend to go in the future.

When the priest proposes a penance to us, in reality he is simply expressing our own desire to show God that we really want to live this reconciliation we have asked for.

SECTION TWO
At What Moment Should a Child Receive the Sacrament of Penance for the First Time?

I. The General Problem

1. Diversity of Customs

All through the history of the Church, very diverse customs have followed one another and many of them exist even today.

- In many countries children receive the sacrament of penance around the age of 7-8, while in other countries they receive it around the age of 11 or 12.

- Furthermore the "penance-eucharist" sequence is not followed everywhere. Certain areas consider it preferable to keep penance until after the eucharist, particularly when the eucharist is received around the age of 7 or 8.

2. Contribution of Modern Sciences

This latter pastoral practice (i.e. penance after eucharist when the child makes his first communion at age 7 or 8) has benefited in the last ten years from the support of various sciences, notably theology and developmental psychology.

Numerous advantages in delaying, in this case, reception of the sacrament of penance, have been brought to the forefront. Let us mention some of them:

- the moral judgment of the child is a little more developed;

- his self-awareness and his intentions are more precise;

- his relationship with God is more personal;

- his aggressiveness and his emotions are a little more controlled.

Let us emphasize that psychologists and theologians agree almost unanimously in admitting that children younger than 9 or 10 are incapable of committing "mortal sin" in the theological sense of the word.

3. Present Situation

There exists at this time a certain confusion concerning the problem of first confession. This is a result of a declaration which came from Rome in 1973 and which lends itself to different interpretations.

If we look back at the balanced reading which a good number of bishops gave of this declaration, we find that it states:

A. The sacrament of penance should be made available to those children aged 7 - 8 who wish to receive it.

B. To assure that this right of the children is a real one, they should receive in the course of their second year at school, before their preparation for the eucharist, a catechesis on the sacrament of penance.

Thus it would be an erroneous interpretation of the declaration to think that all seven year old children should make their first confession.

As one bishop aptly explained it in his pastoral letter on this subject:

> "The General Law of the Chruch promulgated at the IV Lateran Council obliges only those who are conscious of certain mortal sin to seek sacramental absolution in confession. We cannot oblige children to more than the general law of the Church obliges adults. Accordingly, no child is to be coerced into going to Confession."
> (Bernard J. Flanagan, Worcester, Mass., August 16, 1973)

II. Practical Suggestions

1. An Important Distinction

In order to have a balanced educational action, it is imperative to make a distinction between two things:

- formation of a penitential attitude

- preparation for the sacrament of penance.

A. *Formation of a penitential attitude*

The moral formation of a child should include the awakening and the development of a penitential attitude; it is that very attitude which inspires the process of reconciliation.

This formation should begin as soon as the child is capable of understanding what is said to him.

B. *Preparation for the sacrament of penance*

This direct preparation obviously should take place later. But it is very important to understand the following: the greater the vision and finesse with which the moral formation has been carried out, the easier preparation for the sacrament will be for both parents and child.

2. Three Central Affirmations

If we examine the pastoral practice of the Church over the last fifty years, three major aspects become clear:

A. A child, regardless of age, should never be forced into confession.

B. It is the parents, after consultation with the priest who knows the child, who have the final say in deciding whether or not to introduce the sacrament to the child.

C. The sacrament should never be denied to a child who asks for it with the required preparation.

3. How Does This Present Program Encourage the Liberty of Both Parents and Children while still Respecting the Spirit of the 1973 Roman Declaration?

Concretely speaking, we presently find ourselves in a situation which requires that we respect at the same time:

- The child's freedom, as well as his need for moral formation and his right to the sacrament;

- The freedom of the parents who have, in collaboration with the priest, the final decision of whether or not to introduce the sacrament to their child;

- The bishops' freedom to interpret for their respective dioceses the spirit in which the 1973 Roman declaration should be understood.

Being aware of this rather complex situation, the present program has been designed in such a manner that it can be used in several different ways:

A. *For children aged 7-8*

There are two possible cases:

a) You may want to give then a catechesis on penance without preparing then for the sacrament.

In this case, the program should be shared as an intensive experience of moral formation without emphasizing the last stage too much.

The program could be ended:

- either by the family celebration suggested on page 150

- or by a penance celebration without personal confession
  (A suggested model can be found in the pastoral guide for priests and coordinators.)

b) You may wish to prepare your child for the sacrament.

Then you will share in the program with him and emphasize the last stage in order to introduce the sacrament to him.

B. *For children aged 9-12*

There are two possible cases:

a) They have not yet received the sacrament of penance. In this case use the program as indicated, emphasizing the last part in order to prepare them for receiving the sacrament.

b) They have already received the sacrament. In this latter case, you may wish to give them a chance to deepen and renew their approach to the sacrament by living the program; this would be most advantageous, for example, during Lent.

In any case, regardless of the children's age, let us not forget that this is a family program, that is, it provides the whole family with an opportunity to renew itself in its faith and to strengthen its ties.

SECTION THREE
Long-Term Preparation

As we see it the long-term preparation should proceed by degrees in the three or four months preceding the child's actual confession.

What should be done during this time? Two aspects could be emphasized:

- our relationship with the child;

- our relationship with the parish.

1. Our Relationship with the Child

A. *Try to become closer to the child.*

Try to be more concerned with the life of your child. This does not mean, however, becoming more possessive or punitive. Conversely, we should try to understand him better, and share his difficulties and his joys, his hopes, his successes, and his failures.

Try to seek out or to take advantage of opportunities to talk quietly with him, mostly as a listener, but also in order to exchange ideas and experiences.

B. *Place particular importance on certain aspects of family life.*

Take care to deepen family relationships, in particular any experiences of reconciliation that occur. At different times make the religious significance of these experiences clear.

If it is up to you to forgive the child, take the time to experience this fully with him.

(For more information concerning this question, see pages 30)

C. *Invite the child to take part in a celebration of penance with you.*

On one occasion it would be good to invite the child to accompany you, if he so wishes, to a celebration of the sacrament of penance designed for adults or for older children (on the condition that these celebrations are 'alive' and meaningful).

D. *Let the child know that he too can take part in the sacrament later on.*

Tell the child that if he wishes, he can receive the sacrament of penance later on in the year. A special program would help him prepare for it. Suggest that he think about it but avoid talking too much about the sacrament in detail.

What is important is the experience and the gradual unfolding of an attitude of penance in the child's life. An explanation of the rites can easily be given at the end of the program. At this point the child's attention should not be focused on these rites.

Naturally, we should avoid giving any false images of the sacrament: for example the magic concept that it washes and cleans the soul . . . is to be avoided.

E. *Present the program to the child as an invitation.*

About a week or two before the program starts, present it to the child as an invitation made to him by the Church.

Ask him to take some time to think about it before giving his answer.

If the child accepts the invitation, you could suggest that the rest of the family join with him in the program, in whole or in part. In this way they could renew together their christian life and their approach to the sacrament.

This is particularly appropriate if the program is used during Lent.

2. Our Relationship with the Parish

A. *Participating in meetings for parents*

Usually a parish will offer several meetings for parents in order to help them use the program and to discuss with them problems concerning the preparation of children for the sacrament of penance.

There are several reasons why these meetings are valuable:

— they allow parents to exchange ideas and experiences;

— they allow them to deepen and renew within themselves the significance of the sacrament of penance;

— they encourage community spirit, which is necessary for the christian education of the child. This point is so important that there will be a special paragraph on it (cf. division "B").

In cases where a parish has not organized meetings for parents the parents should not be afraid to take the initiative and to seek help from a priest or a catechist.

Parts 1 and 2 of this guide will provide ample material for fruitful discussion. The parents could also prepare together the different stages of the program.

B. *Creating a living christian community*

A warm and living christian community should be created among the families involved in the program, so that all the children can participate in this highly important christian experience.

The program makes constant reference to a christian community which joyously celebrates God's forgiveness. If this community does not exist, the children will have a stunted view and inadequate experience of the sacrament.

A christian community is not born by a decision of some one in authority. It is begun only when people who want it come together to start building it. And the families participating in the program can be singled out as those who can be the creative force of such a community.

C. *Cooperating with the liturgical committee in the parish*

If the parish has a liturgical committee, it is good to work with it so as to assure the children's participation in a liturgy of penance adapted to their needs (but without actually going to confession).

This liturgy could take place in the months preceding the implementation of the program.

Preparations can also be made with the committee for the celebration in which the children will receive the sacrament.

A liturgical committee can be created if none already exists. It is up to the parents to take the initiative in making the parish aware of its responsibility to the children.

PART THREE

Preparation for the Sacrament of Penance

Program for Children of 7 to 8 Years Old

GENERAL VIEW OF THE PROGRAM

— Stage 1: God who gives you life invites you to grow and progress p. 61

- Session 1: God knows me by name p. 62
- Session 2: God calls me to grow and progress p. 64

— Stage 2: God who is love invites you to love p. 66

- Session 1: God calls me to progress in love p. 68
- Session 2: It is difficult to love truly; the Spirit of Jesus is with me in order to help me love p. 69
- Session 3: How we may help one another grow in love p. 71

— Stage 3: God invites you to love him and to pray to him p. 73

- Session 1: Prayer is a way of love p. 74
- Session 2: I prepare myself to pray better p. 75

— Stage 4: God our Father always forgives us p. 76

- Session 1: To come back to God is to return to others p. 77
- Session 2: Together we celebrate God's Peace p. 79

— Stage 5: The Church invites us to celebrate God's forgiveness p. 84

- Session 1: The story of the Good Shepherd p. 86
- Session 2: What you will do in the sacrament of forgiveness p. 87
- Session 3: We prepare ourselves to celebrate the feast of forgiveness p. 89

HOW TO PREPARE THE STAGES AND SESSIONS?

— *At the beginning of each week:*

Take about twenty minutes to prepare the upcoming stage.

- Rapidly look over the pages of the stage in the child's booklet.

- Then go back to your guide so that you have a good grasp of the stage.

- Make a note of:
    the number of sessions,
    the kinds of suggested activities,
    the spirit and atmosphere of the stage.

- Plan ahead the timetable, the necessary materials, etc.

— *The evening before, or the morning of the day chosen for each session:*

Set aside several moments for the preparation of that session, always using together the guide and the child's booklet.

INTRODUCTION TO THE PROGRAM

Important Remark:

As was already explained in the first pages of this book, the program for the 7 and 8 year old group of children can be used for two different objectives:

- on the one hand, to give the child a formation to the virtue of penance and inform him about the sacrament of forgiveness (but without preparing him directly to go to confession);
- on the other hand, to prepare him directly to receive the sacrament at the end of the program.

In both cases the program may be used in the same manner, except for part 5. When we reach part 5 we proceed in the following way:
- If the child does not go to confession but only participates in a family celebration or in a parochial service, we will use pages 41 to 43 as a preparation for this celebration and pages 44 and 45 can be read rapidly.
- If the child goes to confession, we will insist on pages 44 and 45, completing them according to the customs of the parish concerning the sacrament of penance for children.

1. General Perspective of the Program

The program is not a course of studies to be followed by the child. It is an experience that we suggest for you and the child together. It is one of renewed attention to the love of God and his call as seen in our daily life.

A. *Two essential elements of the program*

The first basic tool is... yourself, and your relationship with the child.

The second serves the first: it is the child's booklet, which we present as a path inviting you to walk with the child at his own speed.

That is why the booklet is divided into stages.

B. *The meaning of our task*

In the measure that we are "young at heart" and thus able to live these stages (because God calls us all our life to grow in love!) in the same measure the child will live the experience with us.
As you see, preparing a child for confession is not making him "find some sins" nor "teaching him an act of contrition..." but rather fostering in his life
- a deeper relationship with God,
- a refinement of his moral judgment
- a greater sensitivity to God's invitations in his daily life.

2. Planning of the Program

A. *Duration*

It is suggested that we spend a week on each stage of the program. This is a time rythm which is familiar to the child.

In this case, the program, divided into five stages, would take five weeks. Nothing prevents us modifying this and using four or six weeks for the entire program. Four weeks, however, is a minimum.

B. *What time of the year is suitable?*
— Lent seems the ideal time for many reasons:
- At this time, the child benefits from the support of the whole Christian community living in an attitude of penance.
- The other members of the family, invited to participate in the program, would accept more willingly at this time.
- The child preparing himself for the sacrament now has the occasion to live deeply the spirit of Lent with the family. This creates a happy precedent.

— The program however may be used at any time during the year. Advent would seem specially suitable, but in that case, the program should start two or three weeks before the beginning of Advent so that it can end a week before Christmas.

C. *Content of the program*

Each stage of the program provides pedagogical suggestions and material for two or three sessions a week.
There are two types of sessions:

a) *Individual sessions*

These require an individual contact between parents and child. It generally offers:
- a simple conversation between them with reference to the booklet;
- activities to be performed individually by the child.

These sessions may vary from 15 to 30 minutes.

b) *Family sessions*

These sessions, written with the entire family in mind, usually offer the following:
- a discussion on the child's booklet or family experiences;
- diverse activities: poster construction, pantomimes, games, varied projects, etc.;
- moments of prayer to be prepared and lived together.

The length of these sessions will vary greatly. Usually they are from 20 to 40 minutes.

Any moment of the day, when the family is together, is a suitable time. Time is chosen with care so that each member of the family is happy to be present. Avoid using the hour of a favorite T.V. show.

Each member is free and his participation is voluntary.

3. Spirit of the Program

A. *Atmosphere of respect*

To prepare a 7 or 8 year old child for the sacrament of penance requires tact and delicacy as well as a deep respect for God and the child.

It is easy to become a "traitor" to God by deforming his image in the mind of the child. Because of educational errors at the time of first confessions, many children retain throughout their lives a severe, fussy image of God.

The responsibility of confessors and parents is all-important.

B. *Atmosphere of joy*

Preparation for the celebration of forgiveness should not to be a cause of tension for the child but an experience filled with happiness and joy:
- the joy of discovering a new aspect of God's love for him;
- the joy of a closer relationship with his parents;
- the joy of discovering himself, his talents, and his good qualities;
- the joy of learning to accept himself as he is with his failings and defects without loosing self-respect.

C. *Atmosphere of thanksgiving*

What should be the dominant concern of parents during the program?

- Not to make the child "find" sins...
- nor to make him memorize prayers and "formulae" of accusation or contrition.

But rather
- to bring the child to marvel at the love of God who constantly forgives us and believes in us;
- to give the child the occasion to experience deeply the joy of reconciliation with God and others, first in daily life and then in the sacrament.

We do not prepare the child for an uncomfortable "accusation" of sins, but for a "feast" filled with hope and happy reconciliation.

That is not to say that the confession of sins is not important. If it is prepared in the right atmosphere the accusation is liberating and helps the child to accept himself as he is before God and others.

However the basic atmosphere of his preparation should be one of joy and thanksgiving:

"I have sinned, my God,
but you saved me!
Your mercy is infinite
and I will sing of your love
all the days of my life!"

STAGE 1 God Who Gives You Life Invites You to Grow and Progress

Summary

1. ## Number of Sessions

    This stage is made up of two sessions:
    Session 1:   God knows me by name
    Session 2:   God calls me to grow and progress

    Both sessions may be either individual or family sessions. However, one special conversation must take place with the child participating in the program.

2. ## General View of This Stage

    A. *The call of God*

    Beginning with the child's experience:
    — his joy of life,
    — his desire to grow,
    we present God's call to him as an invitation to grow and progress.

    This invitation is motivated by God's special love for us: it is because God loves us that he invites us to make efforts in order to grow and progress.

    Thus God's invitation is not seen as a compulsory obligation coming from the exterior. It fits into the dynamism of growth itself, which is a fundamental experience in the child.

    B. *Discovering oneself*

    We are all aware of the importance of knowing ourselves. It is a condition for accepting ourselves and feeling comfortable with ourselves.

    But it is also a requirement of our relationship with God: if the relationship is to be truthful, we cannot wear a mask.

It is along our life that we discover who we are, but there must be a day to begin this.

The child ignores himself. Besides being little inclined to introspection, he often is the victim of labels imposed on him by adults. He then sees himself through their eyes with lenses that magnify or deform him. Unfortunately he sometimes even becomes what they say he is. How often a child became lazy, or mean because of constant repetition that he was so!

We will try, in this stage, to help the child know himself in a positive way, that is, to help him become aware of his talents and qualities, so as to lead him to discover gradually the responsibilities entailed. This is far better than stressing defects and fighting them.

3. Pedagogical Remarks

Importance of a personal relationship with the child

The complexity of daily life does not always permit enough time for the individual needs of each child.

This program is an incentive for us to make greater efforts on this point with the child preparing himself for the sacrament of penance.

Right from the start we build on the child's experience of a loving, unique type of relationship between himself and his parents.

It is through this experience that we bring in the idea of a very special, unique love of God for him.

This is one of the reasons why it is important to give the child, right from the start, all the time and attention he needs to live fully with us the various stages of the program.

Session 1 God Knows Me by name

Teaching Methods:

- *Conversation of both parents (if possible) with the child*

- *A moment of prayer*

Remark: This session may take place appropriately at bed time.

1. *Read and discuss with the child pages 2-5 inclusively while recalling every day experiences.*

— Remind him of progress already accomplished during preceding months. We may for example:

- look at former drawing books or writing copybooks and compare with recent work;

- mention things he now performs better, such as putting away his toys, setting the table, taking care of younger children, etc.

— Recall a special occasion when parents were complimented on their children's behavior. Stress the joy and pride they experienced.

2. *Read and discuss pages 6 and 7.*

   a) Recall God's joy as he sees the child progressing.

   - "It is a great joy to God to see you grow and progress."
   - "He gives you life because he loves you . . . ".
   - "He invites you to grow, to become more and more alive and active."

   b) Stress the personal trait of both the love of God and of parents.

   — "You have a special name . . . because you are unique. You are "You"! This is the same for everyone."

   — "Each is called by his name. Each is loved in a special way."

   c) Then speak of memories linked with the child's birth, his Baptism, and his first years of life. Possibly look at old photographs with him.

3. *End with a prayer using the following suggestions:*

   - Father invites everyone to prayer. (A moment of silence for recollection).

   - Mother, then Dad, thank God, each in his own way for the joy of having X... as their child.

   - One parent then recalls God's love for each one as expressed in Baptism: "On the day of Baptism, God called each one of us by name to tell us that he loves us and that we are his children.

     So as to remember this, let us repeat to one another these words of God: "I have called you by name, you are mine."

In a respectful, joyful atmosphere, father takes in his own hands the hands of his wife and says:

"X..., remember that God our Father says to you: I called you by name, you are mine."

Then mother says the same thing to Dad.

Both then take the hands of the child and repeat over again the above words. Conclude with a prayer or a favorite song of joy and thanksgiving or with the following prayer:

"God our Father,
we are your children,
you know us each by name,
we thank you.
We are at peace
because we trust you. Amen.

Remark: If other children participate fully in the program, they also take part and the celebration is longer. Memories of their birth, etc. can then be recalled at table and the conversation would go on during the evening.

Session 2 God Calls Me to Grow and Progress

Teaching Methods:

- *Using the booklet to start a conversation*

- *Personal activities suggested in the booklet.*

1. Read with the child pages 8 and 9 in the book.

    Make sure he understands what he has to do. If you wish you could take a sheet of paper and perform the activity yourself. The child enjoys and appreciates our participation in the project.

2. After the activities are performed, let us read together pages 10 and 11.

    Emphasize that God wants all of us to grow. "Even after our physical self has fully grown, we may constantly continue to progress and grow even more . . . "

    "Mother gradually improves in her cooking. One day, she tried a new cake recipe and spoiled it "a bit". The next time, she tried again and successfully baked a cake which delighted everyone."

    "One always learns . . . we gain skill and ability and acquire speed in all we do."

    Point out the diversity of the talents in the family. Emphasize how we can complete each other and have more fun because of our different abilities.

3. *Conclude with a moment of prayer, drawing inspiration from*

 - the child's reactions in the conversation,

 - the prayers suggested on pages 9 and 11:

 "God our Father,
 thank you for my talents,
 for the joy which they bring me.
 Help me to also use them
 to make other people happy. Amen."

 "I praise you, Lord,
 because it is you
 who gives me life!"

STAGE 2 God Who Is Love Invites You to Love

Summary

1. ## Number of Sessions

    This stage contains:

    - two individual sessions,

    - an optional family session.

    Session 1: God calls me to progress in love

    Session 2: It is difficult to love truly; the Spirit of Jesus is with me in order to help me love

    Session 3: (Optional) How we may help one another grow in love

2. ## General View of This Stage

    A. *Present in a positive fashion God's call to love one another.*

    It is through his experience of love in the home that the child will learn to value love and to discover in this value God's own call.

    Spontaneously, the child, even though he is basically egocentric, enjoys giving his affection and making others happy. We use this fact as well as the example and words of Jesus as a basis for our reflection. Thus we help the child discover in simple daily life the call of God to grow more and more in love.

The "game of joy" will help the child, on the one hand to become more aware of the dayliness of God's call, and on the other hand to experience more deeply the joy of loving others.

B. *Lead the child tactfully towards an awareness of his faults.*

It is joyful to love one another but it is also difficult sometimes. God our Father knows it. He assures us that his Spirit is with us on all occasions.

It happens to all of us to fail in loving others... Just as each of us has talents and qualities which help us to love others in our own way, so we also have our own personal difficulties in the matter. We speak about all this tactfully and simply with the child in order to help him become aware of his failings.

C. *Let us find out together how we can grow in love.*

We must not allow the child to believe that God wants our family to be a "perfect family" without any problems, but rather that he invites us to try and find out how we can overcome the normal difficulties of family life by growing together in love.

This is the topic suggested for the family discussion.

3. Pedagogical Remarks

A. *Personalize God's call*

Help the child understand that as we are all invited to love others, we also have to respond to this call in a personal way, according to our talents and qualities.

B. *Teach the child to think*

Instead of telling the child what to do in the varied situations of daily life, let us help him discover it on his own.

Let us also avoid telling him where he failed but rather lead him to become aware of it himself in God's presence.

Example: When an incident occurs where the child seems to have been particularly jealous, selfish or revengeful let us speak with him about it during the evening.

"Do you remember what happened this morning with X...?

What do you think about it? Do you know why you acted like this?
According to you, what does God think about it?
What could you have done instead to answer his call? Etc."

In the same way we will help the child become progressively aware of the opportunities to love which we miss through inattention or indifference.

C. Place ourself "in the same boat" as the child.

Let the child see that:

- just like him, we try to answer God's call in our life;
- just like him, we also find it difficult at times;
- we need one another to help us grow in love together.

Session 1 God Calls Me to Progress in Love

Teaching Methods:

- *Using the booklet to start a conversation*
- *Drawing*
- *Presenting the "Game of Joy".*

1. Read page 14 with the child.

   Make comments with the help of the following:

   "All day long Jesus had spoken to the crowds of God's love. He had cured many sick people.

   As it had been very warm, Jesus was tired. It would soon be sunset. Jesus said goodby to the remaining people. Just as he was leaving, another group asks to see him.

   In spite of his fatigue, Jesus comes back towards them, takes time to speak to each one and cures the sick.

   It was late in the evening when at last he was able to go home, eat, and rest."

   We may read for ourselves: Mark 1, 32-35
   Luke 4, 31-41
   Matthew 8, 1-18.

   Note verse 40, in Luke 4, "imposing his hands on each one, he cured them." If Jesus were able to cure people as a group, this would be less tiring... but his miracles were not "shows" depicting power. They were signs, symbols of love, a very personal love.

2. *Recall with the child one of his experiences in the joy of loving others.*

   One day, for instance, he made a serious effort to please his little sister. Did he notice the happiness in her eyes? As for him, how did he feel? Let us speak of our own experiences. Then draw the picture on page 15.

3. *Read and discuss pages 16 and 17.*

   Help the child discover occasions during the day when he can:

   • use his talents to serve others;

   • bring joy to other people by his attention and kindness.

   Also mention occasions when we may do the same.

   If we wish we may demonstrate by a drawing, a pantomime, or by using puppets, the situations mentioned above.

4. *Suggest to the child a secret game you can play together until the next session: the game of giving joy to others.*

   This game consists of using kind words and thoughtful acts and of lending a helping hand without being asked, in order to make others smile as often as possible.

   At the next session each one tells about his "adventures in giving joy". Each will benefit from the other's good ideas.

Session 2 It Is at Times Difficult to Love Others
The Spirit of God Is with Us to Help Us

Teaching Methods:

• *Report on the "Game of Joy"*

• *Conversation on the booklet*

• *A moment for prayer.*

1. *Report on the game of joy*

   — Parents and children report on their "secret experiences"...

The aim of this report is not, of course, to "show off" — that is against the Gospel's spirit, — but to profit by others' ideas in an effort to give joy to others.

— Encourage the child to "savor" the special quality of joy he experiences in "giving joy to others".

- "The fun we enjoy when a joke is played on someone or when we eat a delicious piece of cake is a very real pleasure..."

- "The joy we experience when we share the piece of cake to give pleasure to another or when we help mother who is tired... is another type of joy. It is like sunshine in our heart... it lasts longer... it grows in our heart... it makes us more like God..."

- "God's life, his happiness, is to love. It is this life and this happiness he wants to share with us in making us able to love."

2. *Conversation on pages 18 and 19*

— Each one brings out situations where he finds it difficult to love others. Guide the conversation to occasions of daily life when it is difficult for children to get along:

- on returning from school, clamoring for the parents' full attention,

- arguing over T.V. programs,

- getting along together in games, being willing to lend things, doing a fair share of various household chores, etc.

— Emphasize that the Holy Spirit will help us, if we listen to him and if we pray.

3. *Moment of prayer*

Take a few minutes of silence to think about instances when we refused or forgot to love others as God demands.

"Let us pray together:

While remembering moments when we found it difficult to love others let us say the prayer on page 19:

O God our Father,
you give me your Spirit
to help me love.
Teach me to listen to him in my heart. I ask this through Jesus, your Son.
Amen."

"Remembering moments when we experienced the joy of loving others, let us say the prayer on page 15:

My God, I praise you
because it is you who make me able to love."

Session 3 How We May Help One Another Grow in Love

Remark: This session is a family discussion on the joys and difficulties of life together.

Two situations may occur:

a) Only one child takes part in the program: in this case, session 3 will be combined with session 2 in a conversation between parents and child.

We will then make the mobile together, since it will be needed for the celebration.

b) Older children take part in the program. We then use session 3 just as suggested below.

Teaching Methods:

- *Conversation on the joys of living together*

- *Making a mobile*

- *Conversation on the difficulties of living together and the means necessary to face them together.*

1. This step mainly consists in creating a mobile or arranging picture boxes that show the joy of living together.

   Remark: To build a picture box, we paste pictures, photos or drawings on each side of the box. Many boxes may be constructed, then hung from the ceiling by threads and tacks.

   — We remember happy moments from everyday life:

   - an evening playing together,
   - program on T.V. which we all like,
   - picnic or anniversary dinner...
   - surprises, mother's day,
   - constructions in art which we do together, etc.

— We draw incidents recalling the above events, we share in the work, we construct the mobile or the picture box. Words such as "love" or "joy" may be printed. It is advisable to have all necessary materials for the project prepared beforehand.

2. *After admiring the mobile together, we recall the other side of the coin.*

   "It is great to live together... but it is also, sometimes, difficult. There are good and bad days."

   — Show that these difficulties are normal because of traits of character that differ or are too similar, and the necessity of sharing many things, such as the parents attention, room space, T.V., games, etc.

   — Give everyone the opportunity to express his reactions concerning these difficult times.

   According to the number of participants, their age or mentality this is done by

   - simple conversation,
   - skits or sketches expressed by pantomimes,
   - sketches drawn and pasted on poster.

   What is important is that each one may speak, with ease and in an atmosphere of trust, about these difficulties.

   — Discuss together the means to overcome these difficulties.

   - "Some may be solved by a change in home arrangements, the agenda or time table, etc."
   - "Others, resulting from temperaments or individual differences are uncontrolable situations and must be lived with. What is asked of us then is to try and be understanding, accepting, and to find compromises that will allow for common progress."
   - Remaining close to family experiences, it is evident that the discussions should be "realistic"!

   — Emphasize that God does not demand an ideal family without problems. But he does ask us to grow more and more in loving others.

   Remark: Let us not underline moments where all goes wrong because of anger. This is a particular situation to be discussed in stage 4.

   If the atmosphere is favourable, we may end with a short prayer.

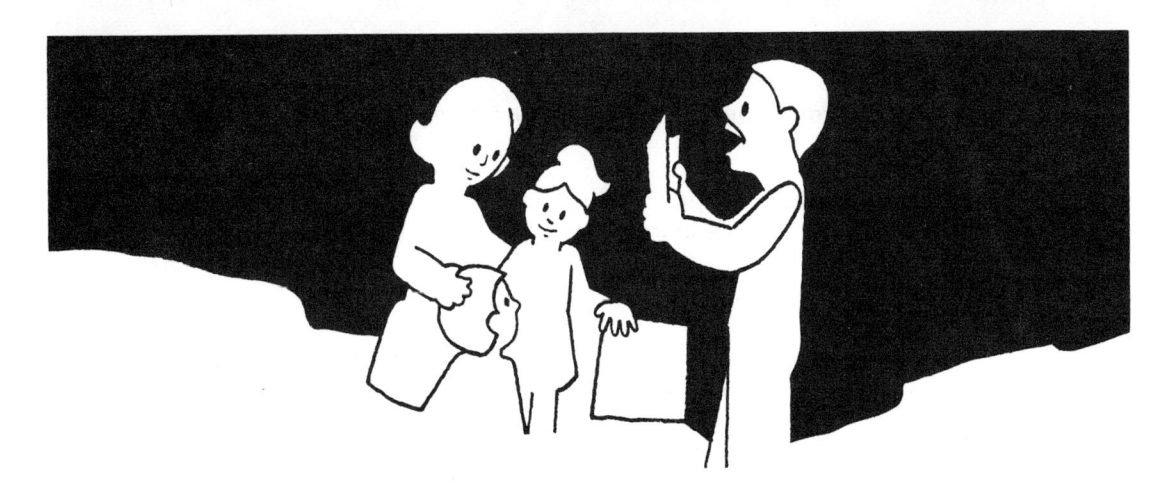

STAGE 3 God Invites You to Love Him and to Pray to Him

Summary

1. Number of Sessions

This stage contains two sessions:

Session 1: Prayer is a way of love

Session 2: I prepare myself to pray better

Both may be either individual or family sessions.

2. General View of This Stage

A. *Prayer as an expression of love*

Starting with Jesus' example and our own testimony, we introduce prayer, not as an obligation but as a normal expression of love and admiration for God. A child once said: "It is I who obliges myself to pray..."

B. *Prayer in our life*

Using examples in the child's booklet (p. 24-25) and our own testimony, we help the child to understand that prayer is possible in any circumstances; it suffices to turn our heart to God.

It is important that the child discover early the joy of God's constant presence in our life.

3. Pedagogical Remarks

A. *Guide the child's prayers to thanksgiving, praise, and petition for spiritual aid.*

We should encourage spontaneous prayer while suggesting the use, at times, of short excerpts learnt or found in the booklet.

B. *Respect the child's freedom*

We must respect the child's freedom, otherwise prayer soon becomes detestable and he'll get rid of it as soon as we turn our back!

What is important is to awaken in the child a personal desire to pray. We can invite him to pray with us, discreetly remind him of praying, prepare or help him to pray and above all pray with him, but we should never force him to pray.

To the extent that God's presence is a reality for us in our daily life, we experience the need and the desire to pray. This will also happen with the child if we help him gradually to discover God's presence in his own life.

Session 1 To Pray to God Is a Way to Love Him

Teaching Methods:

- *Using the booklet to start a conversation*
- *Doing a drawing*

1. Read and discuss pages 20-27 in the booklet.

    — Speak simply to the child of moments when we like to pray to God, to offer Him praise, ask help, tell Him of our love or remain quietly in His presence.

    — Do not be afraid to speak also of moments when we don't feel like praying... Tell the child we pray just the same in these difficult moments, because we love God and wish to tell him so.

    — Make the child understand that when we think of what it really is, we see that prayer is an "extraordinary priviledge":

    "We may at all times speak to God who is so great!
    God loves us so much that he asks us to be his friends and to share with him our thoughts and wishes. Isn't that just marvellous?"

2. *Suggest that the child do the drawing on page 27.*

   Before starting to draw, find together a moment of the day when it is easy for him to start the habit of saving "a minute for God".

   Evening is usually suitable but the child should discover this by himself.

   — Teach the child that if we do not develop the habit of prayer, we will forget about it and thus will not answer God's call to love Him.

   — Suggest to the child that upon rising each morning, it is good to say "Hello" to God who gives us a new day. Little more can be done at that time. But, at least we begin the day with God and afterwards we may speak to him as often as we wish. God is interested in our entire life.

Session 2 I prepare Myself to Pray to God

Teaching Methods: Composing my own prayer booklet or making a poster.

Remark: We can take advantage of this step in the program to help the child acquire the habit of praying in the evening, if he does not already have this habit. The first activity is useful in this respect.

Choose one of the following:

Activity 1: The child's own prayer booklet

— Suggest that the child create his own prayers and write them on different colored sheets of paper. He may also write his favorite prayers.

— He writes one prayer on each page which he decorates to his liking and ties them together to make a booklet.

— During the following days, before bedtime, invite the child to choose an appropriate prayer. Both of you say it together.

Activity 2: A poster

When a child easily forgets evening prayer, ask him to make a poster which he will place on the wall of his room.

This poster can be a drawing such as Jesus praying to his Father, or any other drawing, print, or photo, v.g. Christians praying together, etc. The child can illustrate quotations, prayers, songs, etc. which can be decorated by him as he wishes.

The poster should remind the child of his wish to pray and help him do so.

During the next few days we may use the poster for praying with the child in the evening.

STAGE 4 God Our Father Always Forgives Us

Summary

1. Number of Sessions

This stage is made up of two sessions:

Session 1: To come back to God is to return to others

Session 2: Together we celebrate God's Peace

2. General View of This Stage

A. When we sin, God invites us back to him.

Throughout the program the child has become aware that it happens to everyone to refuse God's call'; this act is called a sin. Now he must learn the process of conversion, of penance, which is God's invitation to us. The first idea to point out is expressed on page 28:

"God our Father always forgives us.
But he demands that we make a move
by coming back to him."

B. What is coming back to God?
Using a story, we will help the child become aware of the three main steps in the process of penance:

- admit our failings,

- come back to others,
- do something to "make up".

We try to explain clearly to the child that:

- returning to others means returning to God;
- when we forgive one another, God also forgives us.

3. Pedagogical Remarks

A. Place of the sacrament of penance in our life

How may we teach the child that the sacrament of penance starts in his life? Let us avoid speaking too much of the future: v.g. "You will receive God's forgiveness..." God does not wait to forgive us. Let us try in daily life to live with the child the varied steps of the process of returning to God: admitting errors, regretting and making up. Let us speak knowingly of the sacrament of penance: "It is not a washing, giving back whiteness of soul," but the celebration of something we live along the days.

B. Choose the proper time for reconciliation

Like everyone else, the child needs to collect himself and calm down before a reconciliation. Let us wait for the "storm to pass" before suggesting a reconciliation. It will then be sincere and serious. (See p. 29 of this guide for reference.)

C. The manner of asking for forgiveness

Many ways exist of asking for forgiveness: a word, a smile, a gesture, a helping hand, etc. Help the child discover these means and choose the one he prefers, regardless of our own ideas.

Let us notice the least sign of forgiveness given by the child. If we insist on a particular sign of reconciliation, when he has already given one of his own, we can spoil the whole procedure.

Session 1 To Come back to God Is to Return to Others

Teaching Methods:

- *Conversation*
- *Making a poster*

It is advisable "to live" this session as a family group.

1. *Read and discuss pages 28-32 in the booklet.*

   When the participants have expressed their reactions to the story, we invite them to recall a similar experience of their own.

   — Speak together about both the difficulties and the joy of reconciliation. The following ideas are useful:

     • Arguments and quarrels are unavoidable.
     • What is important is to forget about them at some point, and come back to others.

   — Have parents and children discuss the difficulties involved in "coming back":

     We don't want to say, "It's my fault."
     We find it hard to take the first step.
     "He'll pay me for that!" we say.
     If I quickly forgive, he'll start over again", we think.

2. *Reflect together on God's call.*

   What God asks us to do is expressed on p. 33.

   He wants us to be reconciled,

   • to say "It is my fault",

   • to take the first step,

   • to forgive others sincerely,

   • to render good for evil.

   — Starting with the stories, along with examples taken from family life bring to light:

     • the uneasiness and sadness of the whole family when quarrels linger on and when pouting occurs,

     • the joy of reconciliation felt by everyone, not only those involved.

   — Carefully bring out the following:

     • When we forgive one another, we receive God's forgiveness and peace.

     • Trying to "make up" is the best means of asking for forgiveness.

— We will now talk of incidents from daily life and ways to find "good ideas"

- to "make up",
- to bring back happiness to those we hurt.

3. Activities

   A. *Suggest the following activity:* making a poster to remind each one of God's call to make peace.

   In the center of the poster might be written: "Happy are those who make peace! They are truly God's children."

   Illustrate it by means of drawings and photos of family scenes and events.

   We may add other slogans such as:
   "To return to God is to come back to others."

   Then decide together where the poster will be placed.

   B. *Choose an appropriate moment to ask that the child draw the pictures suggested on p. 33*

Session 2 We Celebrate the Peace of God

Remark: This celebration may take place in the evening before dinner or at bedtime.

The following plan is proposed as an example. The more family creative ideas go into the project, the better.

I. PREPARATION

1. Recall incidents of daily life.

   On the eve of the celebration, parents ask each member of the family to remember an occasion when he was happy because of another's kindness. He then relates the incident briefly on a colored card (cards are already prepared).

   Example:

   "Nicholas lent me his bike all afternoon."
   "Instead of going fishing, Dad helped me fix my electric train."
   "Because Linda prepared dinner, mother and dad could go out Saturday evening." Etc.

2. To prepare beforehand

- a place to hang up the mobile or picture boxes, made in stage 4,
- a short candle for each,
- a large candle, symbol of Jesus' Light,
- a safe way of arranging all the candles near the mobile,
- a scotch tape to fasten the cards to the candles.

II. CELEBRATION

- When it starts, lights are dim.
  Each carries his card.
- Invitation to prayer (by a parent):

"We have come together to-night to celebrate God's love inviting us to live in his light and his peace."

— Song

Choose a song which expresses joyful trust in God.

— **Part 1: We praise God for the joy of loving one another.** (The lights are still dim.)

1. Introducing the Rite

    - The leader asks a child to bring the mobile (or the picture boxes) which remind everyone of the joy of being together. The mobile is placed in the center of the group and the large candle is lit.
    - The leader then continues:
      "When we think of others and love them it is as if our heart and our home were full of light.. a light of love and joy!"

      "Let us recall together moments when a gesture of love from someone brought us light and joy."

2. Rite

    - Starting with the parents (so as to show the children what to do) each one in turn performs the rite.

Example:

Mother reads her flash card: "Because Linda prepared dinner for the little ones, daddy and I were able to go out."

- The leader says while offering Linda a candle just lit at the larger candle, "Because Linda did that for mother the other day, light and love filled her heart and mother's. That gave more light and joy to everyone at home."

- Mother then attaches her flash card to Linda's candle.

- Linda places her lighted candle near the mobile at a predetermined spot, then she returns to her seat.

- This gesture is repeated until each has placed his candle.

3. *Reading*

"Let us listen to the word of God. What we did will help us understand it."

(Reader)

"God is Light.
There is no darkness in him.
He who loves others,
his heart is filled with light.
He then is united with God because God is Light.
He who dislikes his brother walks in darkness.
The light of God is not in him.
Let us all live as children of light." (Adapted from Jn 5; 1 Jn 2; Eph. 5)

After the reading, there is a short time of silence.

4. *Homily (about 3 or 4 minutes)*

Using a dialogue format underline the following ideas:

- "Our candles were all lit, a moment ago, at a large candle. This large candle represents God's light, which is the love he puts into our heart. "The love of God was awakened in our heart by the Spirit of Jesus given to us." (Rom. 5,5)

- "It is God who makes us able to love and who wants to share with us the joy of loving.

For this joy given to us, let us thank and praise him together."

5. Prayer

   "God our Father,
   you share with us
   the joy of loving,
   you give us your Spirit
   which helps us to love a
   little bit as you do.
   We offer you our joy
   and give you thanks for it. Amen."

6. Song of praise and thanksgiving

Part two: We ask forgiveness for our lack of love.

1. Introduction by the leader

   "It sometimes happens that we refuse to love... We refuse to pay attention to others, to help one another, to reconcile ourselves with others."

   "What happens on such an occasion? In our own heart, as well as in the entire family, there is less love and joy... It is as if God's light became dim in our home..."

   (Put out a few candles)

   "For these occasions when we do not walk in God's Light, when we pull away from others and from God, let us ask forgiveness."

2. Prayer: (by the father or mother)

   "God our Father,
   you know very well
   that at times we don't
   want to listen to Jesus,
   days come when we break peace,
   when we pout,
   when we refuse reconciliation.
   Everyone is then less happy.
   For those days we ask
   forgiveness from the
   bottom of our heart."

3. Here we may:

   — sing an appropriate song, v.g. "Lord, have mercy"

   — or remain silent for a few minutes.

We then continue:

*"Our Father,
give us your Holy Spirit
that he may purify our heart.
Let him strengthen our ability to love.
May he help us to walk as children of light.
We ask this through Jesus your Son.*

Together: *"Amen".*

4. *Conclusion of the celebration*

   In this final rite, the extinguished candles will be lit again while recalling the celebration of penance to be held during the following days:

   "It happens to each of us, in turn, to sin, to break God's peace, to dim his light in us as well as around us.

   That is the reason why Jesus asks us to meet together on occasion to celebrate the sacrament of reconciliation.

   In the sacrament, Jesus gives us, through his priest, a sign of his forgiveness. The priest says to each one: 'I forgive you your sins, in the name of the Father, and of the Son, and of the Holy Spirit.'

   We then become stronger to love, to live together in the light and joy of God."

   Light up again all candles.

   Ideas and impressions could now be exchanged. Conclude the service by a song of friendship and joy. Dinner follows the celebration if the service takes place in the late afternoon, but if the celebration takes place just before bedtime then a snack with cake or other goodies could be shared as a sign of joy and friendship.

STAGE 5 The Church Invites Us to Celebrate God's Forgiveness

Summary

1. Number of Sessions

This stage contains three sessions:

Session 1: The story of the Good Shepherd

Session 2: What you will do in the sacrament of forgiveness

Session 3: We prepare ourselves to celebrate the feast of forgiveness

(If preferred, sessions 2 and 3 can be interchanged.)

Remark:
Session 1 can be either a family or an individual affair. Session 2 and 3 are individual sessions.

2. General View of Stage 5

We now come to the sacramental rite proper. We will approach it in three sessions.

A. First (refer to pages 36-40 in the booklet) we present the theme of the Good Shepherd by means of a story inspired not only from the parable of the God Shepherd, but also from other Gospel episodes on the same topic (Lk 15, 4-8; Jn 10, 1-19).

The details of the story tend to emphasize the important aspects of the theme and to awaken in the child an attitude of joyful trust in Jesus.

B. The second session explains to the child what he should say and do in order to celebrate the sacrament of penance (see pages 44 and 45 in the booklet).

C. In session 3 we will pray with the child and together examine our conscience. This is an immediate preparation for the reception of the sacrament (see pages 41, 42 and 43 in the booklet).

3. Important Remark

Two situations may occur in the use of the program:

Situation 1: The program was used merely as a method of moral formation, a way of awakening an attitude of penance. In this case, it leads the child towards a community celebration, without involving him in a personal confession as such. We may then pass rapidly over pages 44 and 45 which deal with details about personal confession. The preparatory meditation proposed on pages 41, 42 and 43 can be made in the family circle.

Situation 2: The program aims at preparing the child to confess his sins personally during the community celebration. In this case we take time to explain thouroughly pages 44 and 45 and answer his pertinent questions.

4. Pedagogical Remarks

A. *Avoid all matter which can worry the child.*

The family atmosphere during this stage is of primary importance. If parents are anxious, worried about small matters, this will influence the child. It is necessary to avoid remarks, or attitudes which can trouble the child such as — obsession with recalling sins anxiety over details of the proper rites — uneasiness towards the priest — and worst of all, being afraid of God.

We will tell the child about the secrecy that is part of the sacrament of penance. Let us assure him that the priest will never reveal his sins to any one.

B. *Wait in joy and confidence for the moment of receiving the sacrament of penance.*

The whole spirit of the program is that of an invitation to celebrate with joy God's forgiveness. It is important, especially during the remaining days, to live fully this spirit of celebration with the child.

Session 1 Story of the Good Shepherd

Teaching Methods:

- *A story*
- *A conversation on the story*

1. Read slowly with the child the story of the good shepherd

   Let him look attentively at the pictures. (p. 36-40).

2. A dialogue follows:

   We exchange impressions and by asking appropriate questions, we help the child to understand what Jesus, in telling this story, is trying to tell us about our own life.

   Bring out:

   - the love of the shepherd (Jesus);
   - the trust of the little lamb who, after its escapade, better understands the shepherd's love;
   - the happiness of the shepherd, of friends, of other lambs when Frisky returns.

3. Make comments on the last paragraphs of page 40, underlining these ideas:

   "It is a joy for God to forgive us. It is a joy for the Church, the large family of God's children, to welcome us in the celebration of forgiveness. When we sin and afterwards see how generously God forgives us, we understand better his love and we want to love him even more."

4. If the child wishes, he may now draw part of the story or, if he prefers, we can end with the prayer on page 40:

   "My Lord Jesus,
   you are my Shepherd,
   you lead me on the way
   to the House of God.
   I love you.
   I believe in you and trust you."

Remark: Let us remember that this story is an adaptation of different aspects of the Good Shepherd theme as it runs through the Gospels. The story serves as an introduction to the two important texts presented at the end:

"Rejoice..." and: "There is great joy in Heaven..."

Session 2 What You Will Do in the Sacrament of Penance

Teaching Methods:

A conversation on the rites of the sacrament of penance

Remark: This is a practical session and directly concerns the rites of the sacrament. The next session is one of meditation and forms the last step in the spiritual preparation of the child. One may start by either session according to the child's disposition or circumstances.

Explanation of Rites

1. Look through pages 34 and 35 with the child.

    Read together, comment, keep in mind what follows:

    "We know that God forgives us in our every day life when we turn to him. However he wants to give us a special sign of his forgiveness. He wants us to hear the priest speak to us in his name about peace and forgiveness.

    When we celebrate with other Christians the sacrament of penance,

    - we together acknowledge that we have sinned,
    - we ask God's forgiveness,
    - we confess our sins to the priest,
    - we celebrate the joy of our reconciliation with God and others.

    We then become closer to one another, stronger in helping one another to grow in love."

2. Show the child that various names are given to this sign of Jesus:

    - sacrament of penance

- feast of forgiveness

- sacrament of reconciliation

- sacrament of peace (point out the title of the booklet).

All those names mean the same thing. Ask the child which name he prefers and why. Use his favorite name from now on.

3. *Read and discuss pages 44 and 45.*

— Explain to the child:

- the steps in the celebration;

- what he will do and say (keeping in mind the customs of the particular parish)

but take special care not to worry him by stressing minute details.

The contact of the child with the priest should be as natural and friendly as possible while at the same time respectful, because inspired by faith.

— Avoid telling the child that he is obliged to tell all his sins. This obligation refers only to mortal sins, which are no concern for this age group (see p.124).

Our only concern when preparing a young child to his first confession is that he express in his own words his genuine awareness of having done wrong.

If he does recall one or two precise incidents, so much the better, but above all he should feel at ease in approaching the priest. That is the reason why the booklet points out that if he doesn't remember his sins when he meets the priest, a general expression of accusation is sufficient: "At times I do not respond to God's call."

— Explain the meaning of the penance suggested by the priest:

- it is a sign of our wish and desire to return to God and grow more and more in his love;

- it can, at times, be a means of making up for our sins, if that has not already been done.

For these explanations, let us adapt ourselves to what has already been discussed and decided upon at meetings held for the parents.

Important Remark:

If the child goes to confession, it is advisable that he know the priest personally. The confessor could be invited to dinner so as to meet the child in his family environment.

In the program director's guide, an entire chapter concerns priest-child relationship. Parents are also advised to meet the priest confessor and exchange ideas with him.

Session 3 We Prepare Ourselves for the Feast of Forgiveness

Teaching Method: A dialogue — meditation using the child's booklet

Remark: This meditation should take place, preferably just before bedtime on the eve of the celebration, in the child's room.

>The whole setting of this meditation should be an atmosphere of prayer, quietness, and serenity.

— Follow the steps in the child's book, p. 41, 42 and 43.

— Slowly read the text together.

— Take a few minutes for silent reflection.

— Exchange ideas.

— Pray or sing together.

— As to no 2 (Remember your sins) which is the examination of conscience proper, some advice can be useful:

- Let us avoid giving the child the impression that his whole preparation boils down to finding sins.
- Already, throughout the program, he has had many opportunities to think about his failings before God. He perhaps has even spoken to you about it, in all simplicity. Now he only has to remember one or two incidents for which he is sorry.

  The text on page 42 is probably sufficient. If not, the following may inspire you, in drawing the child's attention to certain aspects of his life according to your knowledge of his difficulties:

- "Because God loves me, he wants me to grow, to progress, to mature, to develop my talents and good qualities.

  Do I sometimes fail to make the necessary efforts?

- Because God wants to share with me the joy of loving others, he says:

    "Love one another"

    "Forgive one another"

    "Render good for evil," etc.

    Do I sometimes refuse to answer God's call?

- Because God wants to be my friend, he invites me to show my love for him, by thinking of him, by praying to him.

    Do I sometimes forget about God for many days? Do I even refuse to pray sometimes?"

— After paragraph no 3, if the child wishes, we can read again together the story of the Good Shepherd. We could also sing together or listen to a record about joy and trust.

— When saying "Goodnight" to the child, take care to avoid all worries on material or spiritual matters to take place the next day. Leave him in an atmosphere of peace and joy.

— The evening after the child's first penitential celebration, it is advisable to pray with him before bedtime.

    We can read with him the last two pages of his booklet (p. 46 and 47) and give thanks together in whatever way he wishes.

    We will tell him that he can use his book again to prepare himself each time he wants to celebrate the sacrament of peace and also to help him pray in the evening. A special place in his room will be found for his book.

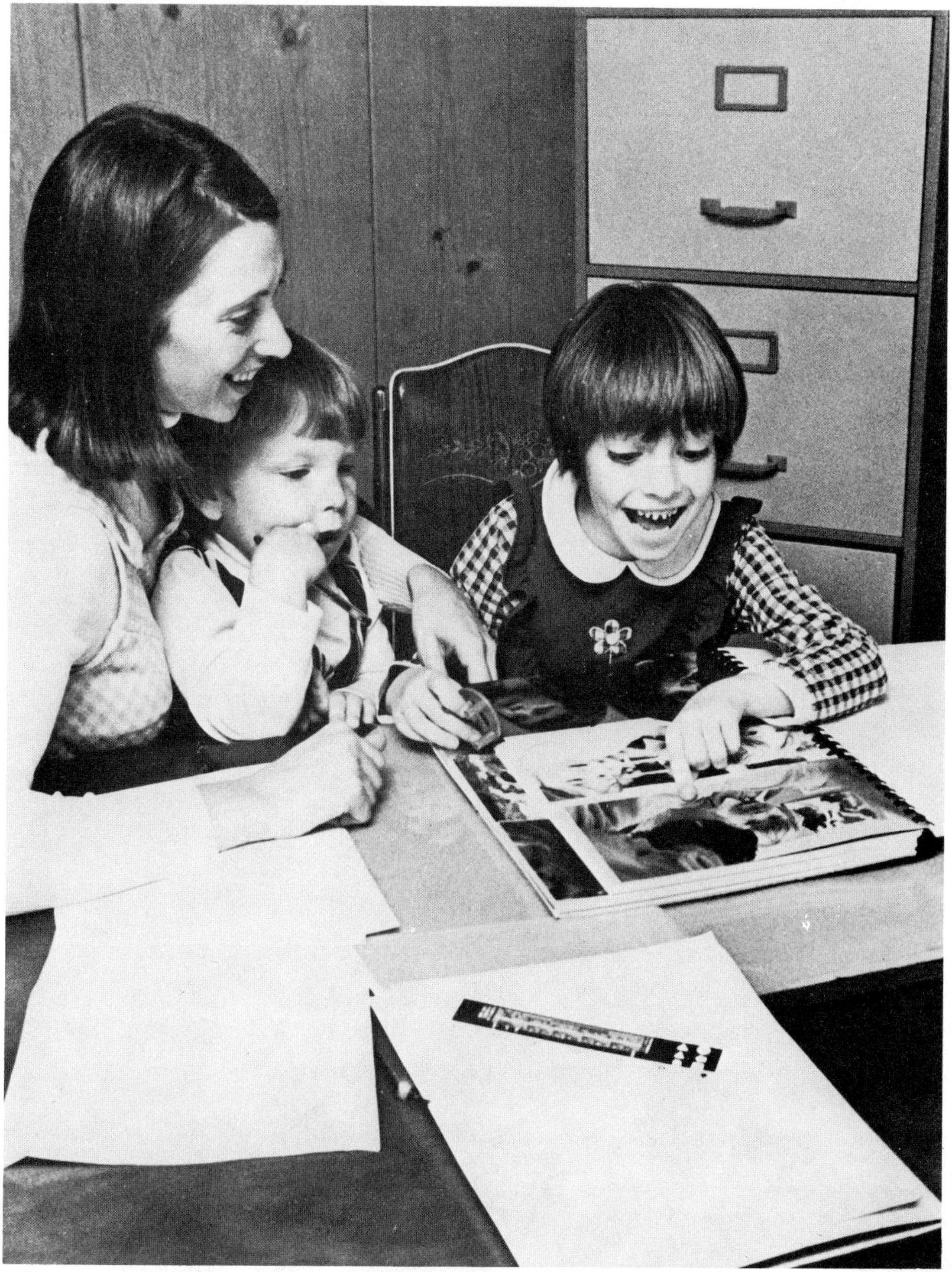

PART FOUR

Preparation for the Sacrament of Penance

Program for Children of 9 to 12 Years Old

General View of the Program

— **Stage 1:** Look at the Lord and see how he loves you — p. 101
- Session 1: We rejoice in God's love — p. 102
- Session 2: Together we celebrate God's love — p. 103

— **Stage 2:** Who are you? — p. 109
- Session 1: God knows me by name — p. 110
- Session 2: Trying to understand myself better — p. 111
- Session 3: The "portrait game" — p. 112

— **Stage 3:** Listen to God's call — p. 115
- Session 1: God is calling me to live and grow in love — p. 116
- Session 2: God invites me to pray to him and to love him — p. 117
- Session 3: As a family we try to respond to the call of God — p. 119

— **Stage 4:** How do you answer God's call? — p. 123
- Session 1: We thank God for all the good we do — p. 125
- Session 2: We are all sinners — p. 126
- Session 3: I reflect in order to know my sins — p. 127

— **Stage 5:** God always forgive us — p. 129
- Session 1: Living together is difficult — p. 130
- Session 2: Coming back to God means coming back to others — p. 131
- Session 3: Celebrating God's peace — p. 134

— **Stage 6:** The Church invites us to celebrate God's forgiveness — p. 139
- Session 1: The Prodigal Son — p. 140
- Session 2: The sacrament of penance — p. 141
- Session 3: Meditation preparing for the sacrament — p. 144

How to Prepare the Stages and Sessions?

— At the beginning of each week:

Take about twenty minutes to prepare the upcoming stage.

- Rapidly look over the pages of the stage in the child's booklet.

- Then go back to your guide so that you have a good grasp of the stage.

- Make a note of:
  .. the number of sessions,
  .. the kinds of suggested activities,
  .. the spirit and atmosphere of the stage.
- Plan ahead the timetable, the necessary materials, etc.

— The evening before, or the morning of the day chosen for each session:
Set aside several moments for the preparation of that session, always using together the guide and the child's booklet.

Important Remarks Concerning the Thematic Pictures In The Child's Book

Each stage of the child's book is introduced by a full-color page illustrating a basic aspect of that stage. The following comments might be helpful for discussing these pages with the child.

The stage 1 picture illustrates an introductory theme on life in general. The other five illustrate a basic theme which is the adventure of a group of children getting together for a common project: the building of a tree-house.

The theme was chosen because it lent itself to the unfolding of various situations whereby the steps towards a celebration of the sacrament of penance could be illustrated. A brief comment on each picture will be found in your Guide at the beginning of each stage.

Introduction to the Program

Remarks:
As already explained in the first pages of this book, the program for the 9 to 12 year old group of children may be used with different objectives:
- *to help the child with his first confession,*
- *to make future confessions more beneficial,*
- *to deepen his moral formation within his daily experiences.*

If we are concerned with a first confession preparation, then part 6 will take on a special importance since it deals directly with the rite of the sacrament.

Let us remember that this is a family program whose success depends largely on the family involvement in the program.

1. General Aim of the Program

The program is not a course of studies to be followed by the child. It is an experience in which you are invited to share.

This experience is one of renewed attention to God's love and to his call as seen in our daily lives.

A. The two main tools in the program

- There are two essential "tools" in the program. The first fundamental tool is... yourself and your relationship with the child.
- The second "tool" is the child's booklet. This is a "road" where you are invited to walk with the child at his own speed.

That is why the booklet is divided into stages.

B. Objectives of the program

a) The first objective is to help the child become aware of the link between his own life and the sacrament of penance. Contrary to what we sometimes think, life is not only a place of sin and the sacrament a place to be forgiven. Life is also a place of God's forgiveness — it is along the way that God calls us to him and reconciles us with himself.

We will try in this program to help the child discover and take the steps that will lead him to a true experience of christian penance in his daily life. When this is accomplished, we will then introduce the idea that the sacrament of penance is the achievement and the joyful celebration of the experiences of reconciliation he has lived through daily events.

b) The second objective is closely linked to the first: it is to help the child become personally aware of his sinfulness.

- that we help him to deepen his relationship with God;
- that he becomes more refined in his moral judgment;
- that his freedom be educated and made more sensitive to God's invitations.

2. Planning of the Program

A. Duration

It is suggested to go through each stage of the program in a week. This is a time rythm which is familiar to the child. The program, divided into six stages, would then take six weeks. Nothing prevents us from modifying this and using five or seven weeks for the entire program. Five weeks, however, is a minimum.

B. What time of the year is suitable?

— Lent seems the ideal time for many reasons:

- At this time, the child benefits from the support of the whole Christian community living in an attitude of penance.
- The other members of the family, invited to participate in the program, would accept more willingly at this time.
- The child preparing himself for the sacrament now has the occasion to live deeply the spirit of Lent with the family.
  This creates a happy precedent.

— The program however may be used at any time during the year. Advent would seem specially suitable, but in that case the program should start two or three weeks before the beginning of Advent so that it can end a week before Christmas.

C. Content of the program

Each stage of the program provides pedagogical means and material for two or three sessions a week.

There are two types of sessions:

a) Individual sessions

These require an individual contact between parents and child. They generally suggest:
- a simple conversation with reference to the booklet;
- activities to be performed individually by the child.

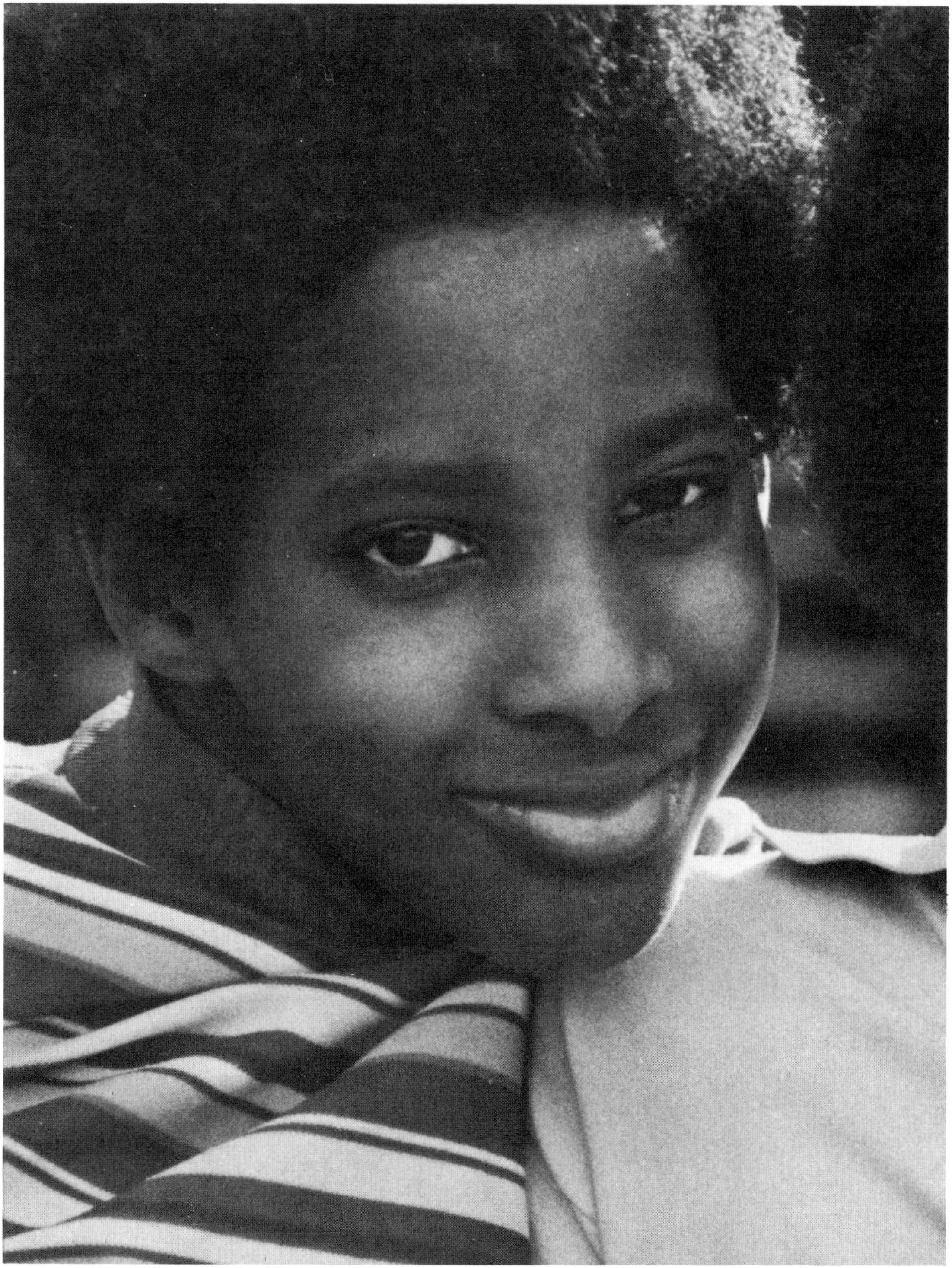

These sessions may vary from 15 to 30 minutes.
As much as possible, both parents should participate with the child in the program. In turn or together parents should experience the sessions with the child.

If other children participate in the program, they use a personal copybook for drawings and projects.

b) Family sessions

These sessions written with the entire family in mind usually offer the following:
- a discussion on the child's booklet or family experiences;
- diverse activities: pantomimes, making of posters, games, varied projects, etc.;
- moments of prayer to be prepared and lived together.

The length of these sessions will vary greatly. Usually they are from 20 to 40 minutes.

Any time of the day, when the family is together, is a suitable moment. Time is chosen with care so that each member of the family is happy to be present. Avoid using the hour of a favorite T.V. show.

Each member is free and his participation is voluntary.

3. Spirit of the Program

A. *Atmosphere of respect*

Pages 2 and 3 of the child's book show in what spirit the program is used. It is a spirit of respect and trust.

The child is not "pushed" into the sacrament of penance. For him as for adults, it is an invitation to be accepted or rejected.

To respect the child's freedom does not mean "do nothing". On the contrary we must "signify" the invitation to the child, and show him its importance and meaning in his life, so that he feels attracted and desires to accept God's invitation.

B. *Atmosphere of joy*

Preparation for the sacrament of penance is not to be a cause of tension for the child but an experience filled with interest and joy:

- the joy of discovering a new aspect of God's love;
- the joy of a closer relationship with his parents;
- the joy of getting to know himself better with his talents and his qualities;
- the joy of receiving help to admit his weaknesses and defects without losing self-respect

C. *Atmosphere of thanksgiving*

What should be the dominant preoccupation of the parents during the program?

- Not to make the child find sins,

- nor to teach and make him memorize ready-made formulae of accusation and contrition.

Rather it is:

- to help the child marvel at the love of God who always forgives us and believes in us;

- to give the child the occasion to experience the joy of reconciliation with God and others mainly in his daily life, and later in the sacrament.

We are not preparing the child for a painful accusation but for a "feast" of reconciliation and hope.

This does not mean that the confession itself has no importance. If it is well prepared, in an atmosphere of peace and simplicity, the accusation of faults is liberating. It helps the child accept himself as he is before God and others.

The basic traits of his preparation for confession are an atmosphere of joy and thanksgiving:

"I have sinned, O Lord,
but you saved me!
Your mercy is infinite,
I will sing of your love
all the days of my life!"

STAGE 1.
The beauty of the world and the joy of people speak to us of God's love.

STAGE 1 Look at the Lord and See How He Loves You

Summary

1. ## Number of Sessions

    This stage contains two sessions:

    - 1st session: We rejoice in God's love

    - 2nd session: Together we celebrate God's love

    Both these experiences can be carried out with the whole family.

2. ## General View of This Stage

    Taking part in the sacrament of penance naturally presupposes an awareness of sin. But in order to realize that we have sinned, we need to come before God and to think about all that his love has done for us. In this manner we come to understand what sin really is. It is an unfaithfulness to God, a deterioration, sometimes a breaking down in our love relationship with God.

    Thus during this stage we should try to make ourselves and the child aware of some of the signs of God's love for us:

    — the beauty of creation

    — the results of man's work

    — the love of those concerned with the child.

    But the main emphasis is on the person of Jesus because it is through him that God reveals himself to us: "Whoever sees me, said Jesus, has seen the Father" (Jn 14,9).

3. ## Pedagogical Remarks

    A. *Deepening relationships with God*

    As we just said, an understanding of penance goes hand in hand with an understanding of God. As God becomes more and more real for us, we become more and more aware of our sinfulness towards him.

    This is why it is important to help the child discover the true face of God.

    This program can help: if we are careful to live it in an atmosphere of prayer, the child will become more attentive to God and will recognize more easily how he is unfaithful to Him.

B. *Learning to give thanks*

> Giving thanks to God is a fundamental christian attitude. It expresses our praise, wonderment, and recognition of God's generosity to us.
>
> The child will have difficulty understanding this attitude if the reality of God leaves us indifferent and "blase"...
>
> Thus we should renew our attitudes, become more sensitive to the many ways God shows his love for us. For example, a beautiful view, a gesture of love, a surprise... are opportunities to express our gratitude and love to God, with the child.

First Session: We rejoice in God's love

Teaching Methods:

- *A discussion of the booklet*
- *Making a poster*

1. Conversation concerning the booklet

— Give the goal of this stage as outlined on page 6 of the child's book.

— Briefly comment on pages 8 and 9 bringing out the following ideas:

- Nobody has ever seen God; but Jesus came to help us learn about God.
- Jesus, by his words and his way of life, helped us understand a wonderful thing:
- God who is so great, so powerful, loves us as a father loves his children.
- He created the world for us.
- He wants us to share in his life and his eternal joy.

— Look at, and read together, pages 10 to 13 in the child's book.

Introduce these pages bringing out the following ideas:

We can understand the love of God our Father:

- by admiring
  - the beauty of the world,
  - the power which God has given man;
- by discovering all the love which is around us.

— Have a discussion on these topics:

- what each one likes best about the beauty of the world, about the things that man does;

- what each person enjoys the most in the joys of friendship, of life together.

2. Making a poster

- Decide together how to make a poster illustrating:

    — the beauty of the world

    — the greatness of man's work

    — the joy of loving.

- Divide up the work.

- In large letters write on the poster one of the texts expressing an attitude of praise which is characteristic of this stage. For example the prayer on page 7 or on page 13, a verse of a psalm, or a song...

Second Session: Together We Celebrate God's Love

Teaching Methods:

- *Preparation of a brief family celebration*

- *Celebration*

A. Preparation of a family celebration

Important remarks

- The members of the family who have decided to take part in the program, should participate actively in the preparation of the celebration as well as in the celebration itself. In dividing up the work care should be taken that younger children are given tasks suited to their abilities. The talents of each person should be used to the maximum: playing the guitar, the flute, dancing, etc.

- The atmosphere of the celebration can enhance its value. Certain elements are necessary for all celebrations:

    — the dignity which comes with faith

    — silent meditation

— a relaxed simplicity.

- Other aspects will vary according to the theme of the celebration. In this celebration, for example, we are concerned with joyous praise.

- A celebration should be carefully prepared in advance so that it unfolds smoothly.

  a) Preparing a place for the celebration

     — Choose a comfortable place in the house where all can gather around the poster which will be fixed to the wall during the celebration.

     — Try to have candlelight or a dim light.

  b) Preparing the readings

     — Choose from among the suggested texts or find others.

     — Let the readers look over the texts in advance. If the readers are children, they should read the selection aloud first on their own.

  c) Preparing songs and prayers

     — Songs should be chosen together and rehearsed if necessary.

     — Prayers suggested in the booklet can be used or others can be prepared.

  d) Preparing the rite

     In a spirit of praise the principal rite will be the offering up of the poster. Other activities such as pantomimes, dances evoking nature, work, or the joy of love can be added.

  e) Choosing the music

     Music can be used to create an atmosphere.

B. *Suggestions for celebration*

   — The greater the role the family takes in creating the celebration, the more beneficial it will be. A basic outline, on which any variation can be made, is given below.

   — The time of the celebration should be agreed upon by members of the family so that everyone is relaxed and happy. The celebration can take place before or after a meal, at the evening prayer, or even on the morning of a holiday if preparation has been made the previous evening.

Celebration

A record or tape can be played at the beginning in order to create an atmosphere of prayer.

1. *Introduction (parent)*

    "We have come together to celebrate joyously the great love of God our Father
    - who gives us life,

    - who gives us the earth for our home,

    - who makes it possible for us to think, to love, and to transform the earth..."

2. *Song of praise*

    Choose a brief and lively one.

3. *Readings*

    The title of the reading should be given by the reader. Choose from among the proposed texts or from a text that the children will understand.

    Choice: A Creation poem from the Book of Genesis or the Canticle of St. Francis of Assissi.

    a) A Creation poem from the Book of Genesis

    In the beginning God created the earth and the sky.

    God said: Let there be earth and water.
    And there was earth and there was water.
    Let there be a sun in the sky for the day and a moon for the night.
    And there was a sun in the sky for the day and a moon for the night.
    Let the fish swim in the water.
    Let the birds fly in the sky.
    Let animals run over the earth.
    And the fish swam.
    And the birds flew.
    And animals ran all over the earth.

    God said: I will make man in my own image,
    in my own likeness.
    And he will have dominion
    over the fish in the sea,
    over the birds in the sky,
    and over the beasts of the earth.
    God saw all that he had done.
    And it was very good.
    And there was night.
    And there was day.

    (Taken from Genesis 1)

b) The Canticle of St. Francis of Assisi

> Blessed are you, Lord my God,
> together with all creation.
> Blessed are you for Brother Sun;
> he is made in your likeness.
> Blessed are you, Lord, for Sister Moon,
> and for my sisters, the stars;
> in the dark sky you make them beautiful and bright.
> Blessed are you, Lord, for Brother Wind,
> for the air and all the clouds.
> Blessed are you, Lord, for Sister Water,
> she is precious, useful, humble and pure.
> Blessed are you, Lord, for Brother Fire,
> with him you light up the night;
> he is beautiful, joyous and strong.
> Blessed are you, Lord, for Mother Earth,
> who nurtures and produces thousands of flowers and fruits.

4. *The rites*

    First rite: Presenting the Poster to God.

    Parent: "Let us now offer to God the poster we have made to show him how happy we are to be alive!"

    The children now bring the poster and hang it up.

    Second rite: Dance or pantomime, etc.

    Using the talents of the family, this joy in living can be expressed by:
    - a dance carried out by one person or everyone;
    - a song accompanied by a tambourine;
    - a pantomime depicting nature, friendship, or any chosen topic.

5. *Prayer*

    — A litany could have been prepared as in the following outline:

    Child: *"For the sun which brings us joy, for water which quenches our thirst."*
        "For..."
    Everyone: *"Blessed are you, Lord!"*

    — Final prayer

    Parent: *"God our Father,*
        you are the creator of the universe
        and of all its wonders.
        You are the source
        of our life and of the love

> which unites us.
> We offer you
> our joy in living
> and growing together,
> we give you praise
> through your son Jesus
> together with the Holy Spirit."

    Everyone: *"Amen".*

6. Final advice and blessing

    Parent: *"In the days ahead,
    let us remember in our hearts
    what God is saying to each one of us
    this evening:
    'I love you with an eternal love,
    my love for you will never end.'
    Let us think about these words
    for a few moments in silence."*

    Blessing: *By both parents together*
    *"May God our Father bless us and keep us
    united in joy and thanksgiving."*

    Everyone: *"Amen."*

STAGE 2.
The group of children performs different activities while one silhouette is singled out in the forefront: "We all have our talents, but each one of us is unique, different from all others."

STAGE 2 Who are You?

Summary

1. Number of Sessions

This stage is made up of three sessions;

- 1st session: God knows me by name
- 2nd session: Trying to understand myself better
- 3rd session: The "Portrait Game"

The third session should be carried out with the family as a whole. For the first two it is optional.

2. General View of This Stage

The preceding stage concluded by praising God, the giver of life. This gift of life, a fundamental reality is now pursued further and the child is invited to explore it more deeply thus increasing his self-awareness.

We are all aware of the importance of knowing ourselves. It is a condition for accepting ourselves and feeling comfortable with ourselves.

It is also a basic requirement in our relationship with God: we cannot be honest with Him if we are hiding behind a false personality...

It is not easy for a child to see himself clearly. Not only is he reluctant to practise introspection but he is often the victim of erroneous labels imposed upon him by adults. He then sees himself through their glasses which magnify or distort his image of himself.

This is why at this stage we will try to help the child see himself as he is, to make him realize that like everyone else he has some talents and excellent qualities on the one hand and failings and faults on the other.

Throughout this study we will try to ascertain that the child keep the confidence and self-respect brought to each one by faith. God tells each one of us that we are precious in his sight, that we are recipients of a unique love: "I know you by name, you are mine" (Is. 43,1).

3. Pedagogical Remarks

  A. *Safeguarding self-respect*

  Helping the child to know himself does not mean leading him to loose his self-confidence. Rather, it means that while helping him recognize his faults and limitations we also lead him to discover his talents and good qualities.

B. Adapting to the temperament of each child

With a child lacking security and faith in his own capabilities, more emphasis is to be put on the discovery and appreciation of his good qualities and talents.

With a child who is over-confident in himself and tends to downgrade others, a better realization of his limits and his faults should be encouraged but without ever hurting him.

C. Show the value of interdependence

The child's attention should be drawn to the interdependence which unites all of us because of the diversity of our talents and our good qualities.

In order to acknowledge without jealousy the talents of others, the child must be made aware of his own talents and also of the need we have of one another.

First Session: God Knows Me by Name

Teaching Methods: • *A conversation between the parents and the child*

• *A moment of prayer*

(A suitable time for this conversation would be in the evening before bedtime.)

1. *Read and discuss with the child pages 14 and 15 of the child's book.* Make clear to the child:

   — the fact that he is a unique person, different from everyone else;

   — the special love that his parents have for him;

   — the personal love that God has for him.

2. *Then recall for him memories associated with his birth, his baptism and his early years.* You could look at pictures and other souvenirs with him.

3. *Conclude with a moment of prayer using the following as a guide:*

   • The father invites everyone to pray.

   • There is a moment of silent meditation.

   • The mother, then the father, thank God in their own words for the joy of having X... as their child.

- Then one of the parents recalls the love God showed each one of us at our baptism:
  "On the day of our baptism God called each one of us, so that he could tell us of his love, so that he could tell us that we were his children. In order to remember this tonight, we are going to say to each other these words of God: 'I have called you by name, you are mine.'"

- In an atmosphere of respect and joy the father takes the hands of his wife and says to her, "X..., remember that God our Father is saying to you: 'I have called you by name, you are mine.'"

  The mother says the same thing to her husband. Then together they take the hands of the child and say the same thing to him: "X..., remember...".

- Finish with a prayer or a song of joy and praise which everyone likes. Or use a prayer such as:

  "O God our Father,
  we are your children,
  you know us by name,
  we praise you,
  we are at peace
  because we have faith in you.
  Amen".

Note: If there are other children who are participating completely in the program, they should take part in this session, which would thus become much longer. Memories of their birth etc. can also be recalled at the table perhaps, and the conversation would take off from there.

Second Session: Trying To Understand Myself Better

Teaching Methods: Individual activities in the child's booklet

Remark: If other children participate in the program, let them use a copybook for their own projects or activities.

1. With the child look over pages 16 and 17 of his booklet.

   - Discuss with him the sports that he enjoys and others where he finds difficulties.

   - Ask him to make the drawing as suggested.

2. *Read pages 18 and 19.*

   Here we do not refer to sports but rather to other talents the child might have. Children often have difficulty recognizing their talents and qualities as well as their failings and errors. We help the child become aware of his talents not so much by telling him what they are but rather by leading him to recall past experiences in which he succeeded. The questions on page 19 help the child become aware of the need we have of one another.

   Ways of helping others are not yet mentioned here. This will come later.

3. *Read together pages 20 and 21.*

   Let us teach the child that everyone has, besides qualities, some defects. There is no question at this point for him to find his own defects. This will be taken care of later. The drawing on page 21 helps us put in evidence what we mean: we are all a mixture of good qualities and defects; this is shown by the use of different colors.

Third Session: The Portrait Game

Teaching Methods: • *A family game* • *A conversation*

1. *Making each other's portrait*

   A. *Suggest to the family that everyone play the portrait game together.*

   First explain the rules and above all the spirit of the game:

   "The purpose of the game is not to criticize each other, but to help us see ourselves better and to understand more fully how others see us. This will help us become the kind of persons we want to be and also get along better with one another."

   It is important that the parents participate in the game and set the mood for it: a humorous and friendly mood!

   B. *Prepare sheets of paper for each person playing the game.* These could be typed in advance in order to save time.

   C. *Play the game together.*

   D. *If everyone wishes that the papers be read and discussed, then care must be taken to ensure that the conversation does not degenerate into mutual faultfinding.*

   If carried out with love and a sense of humour, with a sincere desire to help one another, this conversation can be an excellent opportunity to deepen the simplicity and confidence we have in our relationships with others.

It is up to the parents to "set the tone"; therefore it would be preferable for them to read their papers first to the group.

2. *Making one's own portrait*

— This activity is suggested on page 24 of the child's booklet. It will take place in the days that follow. The child who is preparing himself for the sacrament should be especially invited to participate.

Other participants in the game are told of this activity but are free to join it or not.

— Before making his own portrait suggest to the child that he read over his portraits made by the others.

— If the relationship between parents and children is conducive to such simplicity, each can make his own portrait and discuss it.

3. *Conversation and prayer*

— Choose a suitable moment to speak with the child about the "portraits".

— End with a moment of prayer. The following suggestion may be used:

- Each reads silently his portrait.

- All pray silently.

- Then one parent recites the following prayer or another which inspires confidence:

"God our Father,
you know us by our own name,
you love us as we are.
But you constantly invite us
to grow, progress, and mature.
Give us the courage
to make all the efforts
that are needed to answer your call.
We ask this in the name of your Son, Jesus. Amen."

STAGE 3.
A common project takes form: "Let's build a tree-house!" God's Dream and his call are here symbolized: "That we may come together to build a world of friendship and joy!"

STAGE 3 Listen to God's Call

Summary

1. Number of Sessions

This stage is made up of three sessions:

- First Session: God is calling me to live and grow in love
- Second session: God invites me to pray to him and to love him
- Third session: As a family we try to respond to the call of God

Remark: The third experience is designed for use in the family; the format of the other two is optional.

2. General View of This Stage

In this third stage the child is invited to look once again to God in order to hear his call. Any reflection here is closely linked with the preceding stage. For it is through what we are and what we can become that God summons us.

Before giving any precision about God's call we present it as an invitation to share in God's Dream. This Dream can be expressed as follows: that all men may share in God's own joy by building a world of love (p. 26-27 of the child's book).

The stage then unfolds as follows:

- We first stress God's wish that we all fully develop our talents and good qualities (p. 28-29).
- We then indicate the two major directions of christian life and growth:
  - to serve others (p. 30-33)
  - to love and praise the Lord (p. 34-35)

The stage ends with a presentation of some "words of God" that express his call (p. 36-37).

3. Pedagogical Remarks

A. Morality should be presented as an invitation by God and not as a series of laws.

Avoid giving the child a list of commandments. Rather invite him to listen to the call of God which reaches him in his daily life.

B. *Encourage initiative and freedom on the part of the child.*

Try to avoid telling the child what he should do; invite him to discover for himself what God wants of him.

Little by little help him understand:

— that we have a responsibility toward our talents and our good qualities;

— that during our entire life we must try to discover what God is calling us to.

At the opportune time, pray with the child and ask the Holy Spirit to help you both understand God's call.

Remark: If there are other children taking part in the program, the conversation should be conducted in a group setting, then each child can do the individual activities in his own drawing book.

First Session: God Calls Me to Live and to Grow in Love

Teaching Methods

- *A conversation*

- *Personal reflection and activities*

1. *Read and discuss pages 27, 28 and 29 with the child.* Then let him think about it and answer the questions on page 29. In the course of the discussion help him become aware of the precise efforts he has to make in order to develop his talents and good qualities.

    It could be helpful to read over with him what he wrote on pages 18, 19, 24 and 25 of his booklet.

2. *Read and discuss with him pages 30 to 33.* Help him in particular to grasp the following ideas given on page 32:

    "God asks all of us to help build friendship and joy. But because of our particular talents and qualities, each one of us has to answer this call in a special way, different from everyone else."

    Take examples from family life to help the child understand this better.

3. *Give him time for reflection and for answering the questions.*

    Then let him do the drawings suggested on pages 32 and 33. When he has finished, discuss his drawings with him.

Second Session: God Asks Us to Love Him and to Pray To Him

Teaching Methods:

- *Using the booklet to start a conversation*
- *Making a cartoon strip*
- *Personal reflection and activities*

1. A discussion

    Read and discuss with the child pages 34 and 35 of the booklet: "God invites us to become more and more his friends."

    In the course of this discussion:

    - try to avoid presenting prayer as an obligation imposed upon us;
    - try to help the child understand that when we really love God, when we understand all that he has done for us, we feel a need within us to pray to Him. As one boy said, "I do it because I need to."
    - Help the child to consider what time of day should be best for him to spend a few moments with God in prayer. The evening is often the best time, but the child should discover this on his own.
    - Invite him to talk about the eucharistic celebrations and his catechism classes:
        — in order to see any difficulties he may be having;
        — in order to see how he can fully benefit from these two special encounters with God.
    - Don't talk about Sunday obligation in terms of mortal sin, but say rather that the Church asks us not to miss this celebration unless we have a very good reason.

2. Making a cartoon strip

    Ask the child to make a series of drawings telling the story on page 34.

    - Jesus left his friends' house before sunrise.
    - Everyone was looking for him . . .
    - Finally they found him, he was on the mountain, praying to his Father in the peace of dawn.

    Suggest that he write under the cartoon Jesus' invitation to us: "You too pray to the Father." If he wishes he can say how he plans to do this.

3. *Personal reflection and activity*

   Some other time, read and discuss with the child the words of God on pages 36 and 37.

   Invite him to make the poster as suggested on p. 37. Suggest that you might join him in the evening during this week, to discuss one of these "words of God" proposed in his booklet. If he likes the idea you could proceed as follows when you meet:

   - One of you chooses a quotation and reads it aloud.

   - Both think about it for a few moments in silence.

   - Then exchange ideas about it.

   - End with a spontaneous prayer or the one suggested in the booklet:

   "Lord Jesus,
   you came to tell us
   of the Father's love
   and to help us hear his call;
   open my heart to your Word
   so that I may answer it with love."

Third Session: Trying to Discover How Our Family Can Answer the Call of God

Teaching Methods:
- *Time for prayer and discussion in the family*
- *Making a poster*

Important Remark:
We suggest hereafter two themes of discussion:
- the first deals with the responsibility of the family as a group concerning love and service of others;
- the second deals with the life of prayer within the family.

These suggestions can be used in two different ways:
- one theme can be discussed during the program and the other one later on during the year;
- both themes can be discussed at different times in the course of the program.

   1. First theme: The Responsibility of the Family Concerning Love and Service of Others

   The purpose of this discussion is to try and answer together the following question: As a christian family what is God asking us to do?

   This is not so much concerned with internal relationships in the family within the home, but rather with the attitudes and responsibilities of the family group towards the external world.

   A. Moment of prayer

   — The parents announce a family meeting to which all are invited. Together the family decides on a suitable time.
   — At the beginning of the meeting one of the parents clearly outlines the purpose of the get-together, then invites the family to meditate for a moment and directs the prayer along the lines of pages 26 to 30: The Dream of God.

   Here are several suggestions:
   - "We know about God's Dream: that all men will share his joy and learn to live together in love."
   - "He is calling each one of us, you X..., you Y... He is calling me to help him bring about his Dream."
   - "But he also asks each christian family to do something together to help him achieve his Dream."
   - "Thus today let us try to discover how we as the X... family can better answer the call of God."

   Then everyone can pray to the Holy Spirit, either in silence or aloud together.

B. *Discussion themes*

Here are several points for reflection:

- a. Let us ask ourselves about our family attitudes towards our relations and friends: grandparents, aunts and uncles, friends...
    - — How do we try to love them?
    - — Are there some who especially need our friendship because they are alone, sick or in difficulty, etc.?
    - — How can we love them better?

- b. Let us ask ourselves what role our family plays in the life of the neighbourhood:
    - — How do we get along with our neighbours?
    - — How do we fit into the life of the neighbourhood?
    - — What are our cares and responsibilities in view of the problems of the neighbourhood?
    - — What can we do as a family?

- c. In the real world today there are great problems that concern everyone:
    - — ecology
    - — the fight against poverty and hunger
    - — political problems in our daily life
    - — mutual aid during a disaster, etc.

    Let us ask ourselves what our responsibilities and reactions are to these problems.

C. *Concluding the discussion and making a poster*

- a. Concluding the discussion

    Be aware of the practical conclusions and decisions that come out of the discussion. Then divide up the responsibility for putting these into practice.

- b. Making a poster

    - If you wish the results of the family's discussion can be expressed in a poster. In the center, a short text on the Dream of God or words from the Bible or anything else which tells of God's call can be printed. Around this the decisions made together can be illustrated in print or by drawings.
    - Finally end with a moment of prayer offering God the decisions taken by the family and asking his help in putting them into action. The prayer found on page 30 would be suitable here:

    *"Lord Jesus,
    you are the One
    who came to tell us
    about the Dream of God;
    give us your Spirit
    so that all together
    we may help his Dream
    come true."* Amen.

2. *Second Theme:* The Life of Prayer Within The Family. Prayer life in the family is also a way of answering God's call and of helping others to do so.

   We may want sometime, now or later during the program or during the year, to think together about this topic of prayer. If so, proceed just as you did with theme one.

   Here are suggested items:

   a. Question ourselves on the life of prayer in the family:
      - Is our family prayer life adapted to the needs and wishes of everyone?
      - What could we do to make it a more lively, helpful family prayer?
      - In our family prayer effort do we respect the freedom of each member?

   b. Question ourselves on the part we take in our parish liturgies:
      - Are these lively and beneficial?
      - If not, what can we do to enrich and update them?

   c. Question ourselves on what we can do in the neighborhood:
      - Are there neighbors who would enjoy at times praying with us?
      - If so what can we do to answer this need?

STAGE 4.
It is difficult to love one another and to cooperate... sometimes we don't want to do it, we quarrel and fight, we drop out, we turn away from one another...

STAGE 4 How Do You Answer God's Call?
Summary

1. Number of Sessions

This stage is made up of three experiences:
- First session: We thank God for all the good we do
- Second session: We are all sinners
- Third session: I reflect in order to know my sins

— The first session is for family use. The other two should provide opportunities for a very personal conversation between the child who is preparing for the sacrament and one of his parents (or even both).
— If other children who have already made their first confession are taking part in the program, the necessary time to read and discuss the same pages of the booklet with them should be taken.

2. General View of This Stage

This stage leads the child more directly towards an examination of conscience. Having been encouraged to listen to God's call, the child is now invited to evaluate the quality of his response.

Let us look at the title: "How do you answer..."

Because it is a question it opens the way to several possibilities. And this is why:

Normally when we speak of an "examination" of conscience, we think of "sin". Actually this is too restrictive an interpretation: our conscience does not make us aware only of failings, it also takes into account our good actions, actions which have value...

It is this aspect to which the child should first direct his attention. He should be asked to recall different times when he behaved like God's friend. This should be done not to give him a sense of personal pride but rather to give thanks to God who lets us say "yes" to his call (p. 40 and 41).

Thus having looked at himself positively — which naturally should give him a sense of security and confidence — the child can now consider the other side of his response, i.e. his unfaithfullness (p. 42 and 43).

This unfaithfulness sometimes manifests itself in actions which are easily spotted because they are definite and deliberate acts: for example, a revengeful act, stealing, lying, (p. 46).

But there is also a kind of unfaithfulness that is the result of repeated actions which the child has more difficulty in seeing such as bad habits. This is often more serious because these repeated acts often serve as a pathway leading to main directions we take in our lives. Using an example, we suggest that the child try to find some habits which he is developing and which little by little might separate him from God (p. 47).

This section concludes with several remarks on intent and temptation (child's book p. 48-49). We are sinners before God not because we are tempted to do wrong (temptation), but because we decide or will ourselves to do wrong (intent). These two distinctions are made clear to the child in the light of the biblical saying: "God knows our hearts."

3. Pedagogical Remarks

A. *Avoid stereotyped lists of sins*

Giving the child a list of sins, from which he only has to choose a few, may seem the easiest way to prepare him for confession.

But this method has serious drawbacks:
- You run the risk of developing in the child a legalistic mentality concerning what is permitted and what is forbidden.
- God's call to us and our refusal to answer to it become depersonalized: the things which the child knows he has done wrong, in his own life, may not necessarily be on the list... Furthermore just reading the list may make him feel that he is guilty of sins which he has not committed.

What is important in a child's confession is not that he remember every sin that he has committed. Rather it is better that he is truly sorry for some wrong thing that he has done and of which he is aware, in other words that he realizes he has sinned and wants to ask for forgiveness.

B. *Must we speak of mortal and venial sins?*

It is not necessary to go into this distinction when preparing a child for his first confession. You run the risk of creating within him a state of anxiety, which could damage the entire atmosphere of his preparation for the sacrament.

Later on in the months that follow, when he has been to confession at least once more there will be time to do this. Here are suggestions to approach the matter:

a. Point out that in our lives certain wrongdoings are more serious than others:

v.g. • to keep deliberately a grudge against someone;
• to decide to be revengeful and watch for an opportunity to get even;

- to refuse deliberately to help soneone who is in real necessity;
- to lead someone astray and bring him to do something very wrong or dangerous for him or others;
- to decide deliberately not to be God's friend any more, etc.

These actions are very serious because in doing them, we deliberately turn away from God. When we willingly displease him like this in something very serious we break our friendship with him. It is now dead on our part. This is called a mortal sin.

God however keeps on loving us. He is willing to forgive us. He invites us to come back to him through the sacrament of penance and to make up for our sin.

b. Clarify the question of personal involvement:

It may happen that we do something seriously wrong but without being completely aware of it or without having really wanted to do it... In such a case we do sin, but our friendship with God is not broken, these actions are called venial sins.

The less serious sins we unfortunatly commit in our daily lives are also called venial sins.

c. Underline the necessity of confessing mortal sins:

If we were to commit a mortal sin, the Church asks us to go to confession before we celebrate the Eucharist.

She demands this effort as a sign of our repentance and of our desire to come back to the Lord.

First Session: We Thank God for All the Good We Do

Teaching Method: Making a poster

This experience is essentially the construction together of a poster or a film (or comic strip) showing moments when, thanks to someone's efforts, everyone is happy.

1. *Read and discuss together as a family pages 40 and 41.*

2. *Try to remember together good times when everyone in the family was happy through the efforts of others.*

    — Recall precise occasions:
    - a family feast was prepared by all,
    - a general project such as a yard or family-room effort,
    - a picnic joyfully shared,
    - an evening of activities with participation by every member of the family, etc.

- Recall concrete gestures of friendship and help:
    - When Mother and Dad want to go out, the older children babysit at night... They even prepare dinner.
    - Once, Dad refused to go fishing in order to fix the washing machine.
    - Nicholas lent his bike to Anthony on Saturdays for the entire forenoon.
    - Marylyn took the younger children to the bazaar...

3. Try to further illustrate these moments.

4. Admire and discuss together the poster or the film. Write above it a prayer of thanks.

5. Together pray for a moment giving thanks for the love and the joy that the family has shared.

Second Session: We Are All Sinners

Remark:

This experience, like the one following, is simply created to give the child a chance to have a heart-to-heart talk with his parents.

- Here it is not yet a question of a complete examination of conscience, but rather reflecting together on christian life, its demands and its difficulties.

- It is important that the child realize that we are all in the same boat and that we too need to meditate and to pray in order to place our life before God.

Teaching Method: Using the booklet to start a conversation

1. Try to find a good time for this conversation and read with the child pages 42 to 45.

2. Discuss concrete examples taken from the life of the parents as well as from the life of the children.

3. If you wish, conclude with a moment of prayer as suggested below:
    - A moment of silent reflection, thinking about our life in God's presence. Reading over page 42 might be helpful.

    - A common prayer, spontaneous or inspired by the one on page 51:

    "O God our Father,
    you are always ready
    to forgive us,
    we give you thanks and praise,
    and in you we put all our trust."

Third Session: Through Reflection I Can Better Know My Sins

Teaching Method: Using the booklet to start a discussion

1. *With the child read pages 46 and 47.*
   Then without talking specifically about his or your sins but in order to get examples of things which could happen at home, at school or elsewhere, ask him about:
   — specific actions which one can easily see are wrong;
   — habits which little by little can lead us away from God and the others.
   Give some examples taken from family life or the professional life of the adults in the family.

2. *Read and discuss in the same way pages 48 and 49.* With the help of concrete examples, once again taken from the children's life or the life of the adults, help the child to better understand the following:

   - *Our intentions can change the value of an act.*
     Be sure to emphasize that we cannot judge others. Only God knows what each person holds in his heart.

   - *There is a difference between temptation and sin.*
     Make it clear that everyone at sometime is tempted to do wrong. God knows this and understands this; he is there to help us; this is why we ask his help in our prayers.

3. *This conversation can be concluded by a moment of prayer.*

   Remark:
   If the program is being used as a renewal program for a child who has already celebrated the sacrament, it could be appropriate here to discuss with him the question of mortal and venial sin. Refer in this case to the Pedagogical Remarks "B" of this stage.

STAGE 5.
God invites us to come back to Him by coming back to one another, by being reconciled with one another.

STAGE 5 God Always Forgives Us
Summary

1. Number of Sessions

This stage is made up of three experiences:
- 1st session: Living together is difficult
- 2nd session: Coming back to God means coming back to others
- 3rd session: Celebrating God's peace

It would be best if these three experiences were shared by the whole family. In cases where the whole family cannot come together, suggestions offered here should be adapted to the situation.

2. General View of This Stage

This stage — the longest in the booklet — is in one sense the most important because it helps make the sacrament a reality in daily life: in effect, the purpose is to show the child that God is always willing to forgive us and that we can ask His forgiveness whenever we want.

However, asking God's forgiveness does not consist in just a simple formality, or verbal declaration; rather it means taking deliberate steps which involve us completely.

We will explain this to the child in outlining to him the demands of such an undertaking:

"Coming back to God" means:
- agreeing to say: it's my own fault (p. 52-53);
- coming back to others (p. 54-57);
- doing something to show we are sorry (p. 58-62).

Furthermore we are not alone in this: the Spirit of Jesus is with us to help us make up for our sins (p. 63).

The last two pages dealing with this stage are designed to strengthen the child in his confidence in God: no matter how far afield we may wander, God is always ready to welcome us back and to trust us again, as the story of Peter shows (p. 64-65).

3. Pedagogical Remarks

A. Make the sacrament a part of life

How do we help the child see that the sacrament begins in his life right now?

- First of all try not to use words that deal primarily with the future: for example, "You will receive God's forgiveness"...
  God doesn't wait until we have received the sacrament of penance to forgive us.

- Using things that happen in his everyday life, help the child to live or experience the different steps we take towards reconciliation with God: recognizing our faults, feeling sorry for them, making up for our sins.

- Try to speak properly about the sacrament: it is not a kind of bleach which will whiten our soul, but the celebration of something we are trying to live each day.

B. *Choosing the right time for reconciliation*
Like everyone else, a child needs time to calm down before he is able to forgive or to ask forgiveness. Allow time for this period of aggressiveness to pass by before suggesting that he be reconciled: this will give him the opportunity to think about what he wants to do and to do it more willingly and sincerely.

C. *How should we ask for forgiveness?*
There are many ways to ask for forgiveness: a few words, a smile, a gesture, doing a favour. Help the child to discover that all these are possible alternatives and help him to choose the one he would like without imposing your own way on him.

Above all, be very sensitive to the smallest signs of forgiveness given by the child: if you try to force him to show forgiveness after he has already said he was sorry in his own way, you may well spoil everything.

First Session: Living Together Is Difficult

Teaching Method: A family discussion on life together, accompanied by pantomimes or drawings.

1. *Look at the poster about the joy of life together (stage 4, first session), talk about it again for a few minutes.*

2. *Then turn attention to the other side of the coin:*
   "It is wonderful to live together... but it is also very difficult... There are good days and there are bad days."

   First stress that these difficulties are normal; they often come:
   - from too different or too similar traits and tastes;
   - from the necessity of sharing so many things, the environment and facilities, T.V., games, parental attention and affection, etc.

- Ask each person to express his ideas on these difficult times. Depending on the number of participants, their ages and capabilities, this can be done by:
  — a simple conversation
  — short rapid pantomimes
  — little drawings which can be pasted onto a poster...

  What is important is that there is an atmosphere of mutual confidence in which to discuss these difficulties.

3. *Finding ways to overcome these difficulties*

   - Certain ones can be easily overcome by changing the organizational set up or the schedules, etc.

   - Others which are the result of personality conflicts, situations which cannot be changed, constantly recur and we must try to solve the problems through understanding and accepting each other or by trying to compromise. This should be discussed realistically in terms of family experiences.

   - Make it clear that God is not asking us to be an ideal family without any problems at all. He is asking us to try together to progress and grow in love.

     Note: Times when there were serious difficulties and people got very angry, should not be discussed today. These will be discussed in the second session.

4. *If the atmosphere is conducive to it, end with a few minutes of prayer.*

Second Session: Coming Back to God Means Coming Back To Others

Teaching Methods:
- A family discussion, possibly accompanied by pantomimes
- Making a poster
- Using the booklet to start a conversation

Note: If other members of the family are not participating, then the discussions can be carried out while you and the child are looking through his booklet.

1. *A family discussion concerning what it means to "come back to God"*

   The purpose of this discussion is to help the children understand the dynamics or the steps involved in conversion. This is clearly explained in the headings on pages 52 to 59 of the child's booklet.

   It would be good to have these headings written on strips of paper so that they can be hung up on a wall as the discussion progresses.

"Coming back to God means:
- agreeing to say: "It's my own fault",
- coming back to others,
- doing something to show we are sorry."

A. *Begin the discussion using the text on page 50.*

   Call to mind the really difficult times mentioned in the first learning experience.

   Bring out the following ideas:
   - It is inevitable that there will be quarrels, fights, etc.
   - What is important is to forget about them at some point and to ask each other's forgiveness.

B. *Have parents and children discuss the difficulties they find in "coming back"... forgiving... being reconciled...*

   - No one wants to say: "It was my fault".
   - No one wants to take the first step...
   - Everyone wants "to make him pay for that!"
   - Everyone says: "If I forgive him too quickly, he'll just start everything all over again..."

C. *Think together about what God is asking us to do.*

   Read and discuss pages 52 to 57 of the child's booklet.
   Bring out the following ideas:

   — "Admitting... recognizing the things we have done wrong, saying "it's my fault"... is a courageous thing to do. It makes a person greater in the eyes of God and in the eyes of others."

   Hang the first saying on the wall:
   "Coming back to God means
   agreeing to say: it's my own fault."

   — "God asks us to be the first to bring about a reconciliation:
   - by taking the first step,
   - by being good to others even when they are mean to us,
   - by sincerely forgiving."

   — Using the story on pages 55 and 56, and with examples taken from family life, bring out the following:
   - the embarrassment and sadness which the whole family feels when someone is holding a grudge, sulking, etc.;
   - the joy the whole family feels when there is forgiveness and reconciliation.

D. *Make certain that the ideas expressed in pages 54 to 57 are very clear:*
- Coming back to others means coming back to God.
- When we forgive each other, we receive God's forgiveness and his peace.

Hang up the second saying:
"Coming back to God means coming back to others."

2. *Making a poster*

— Suggest to the family that they make a poster which will help them remember what God is asking them to do when things become difficult.

— In the center of the poster could be put a quotation from the Gospels, for example:
"Happy are those who make peace!
They are truly children of God."

— The poster can be decorated according to the desires and choices of the group and together they can choose the best place to hang the poster. The poster could also be decorated with scenes illustrating the joy of reconciliation: actual or imagined events.

— The headings which were put up previously — coming back to God means... — could be placed around the poster.

3. *Using the booklet to start a conversation*

A. *At a different time on this day, or on the next day read and discuss together pages 58 to 63.*

— Read the story of Zacchaeus, pp. 58-59.
Point out that the best means to ask forgiveness is to do good to the one offended.

— Read the two other stories as examples adapted to children's life (pp. 60-63).

— Recall similar occasions and events in family life.
Remember specially the joy we experience when, because of us, another smiles again.
As to Margaret's story, notice how she made sure that she would not be forgetful again. She decided to pray before taking up her picture book.

B. *One evening during this week, put aside moments to read and talk over with the child pages 64 and 65.*
Bring out the fact that we at times hate to give back our trust to someone who hurt us. But God is forever ready to forgive and trust us.

Third Session: Celebrating God's Peace

Note: This celebration could be used as the evening prayer when everyone is together, either before supper or before going to bed.
The proposed outline is only a suggestion. The more a family is involved in arranging the celebration, the better the celebration will be.

CELEBRATION
— **Opening prayer**
(Leader, parent)
"We have come together this evening to celebrate God's forgiveness and peace. God is continually giving us his forgiveness and peace when we try to bring about reconciliation among one another..."
— **Song**
Choose a song which shows our faith in God's love and concern.

— **First reading**

- Introduction:
"Let's listen to the words of two friends of Jesus, Paul and John, as they tell us what God is asking of us."
- Reading:
"Don't make the Holy Spirit unhappy by becoming angry.
But if you do get angry, don't let
the sun set on your anger.
Be compassionate and kind to each other, forgive each other as
God forgives you.

Try to be like God, you are his children.

Try to walk in the ways of love, as Jesus did.

As children of light, walk in the paths of goodness, justice and truth.

Then, you will be one with God
and you will be united with each other,
because God is Light,
and God is Love.

Beloved, if God loves us so much,
we too should love one another."
(Taken from Ephesians 4 and 5 and 1 John, 1 and 4).

- Reader: "End of the first reading."

- Everyone: "Thanks be to God."

- Leader:
"Let us pause for a few moments and think about the words of God."
Have a few moments of silence.

— Second reading

- Introduction
"Let's listen as Matthew tells us what Jesus did for two blind men."

"As they went out of Jericho, a great crowd followed Jesus. And behold, two blind men sitting by the roadside, when they heard Jesus was passing by, cried out, "Have mercy on us, Son of David!"

The crowd rebuked them, telling them to be silent; but they cried out all the more, "Lord, have mercy on us, Son of David!"

Jesus stopped and called them, saying, "What do you want me to do for you?"

They said to him, "Lord, let our eyes be opened."

And Jesus in pity touched their eyes, and immediately they regained their sight.

And they began to follow him."
(Mt. 20: 29 to the end)

- Reader: "This is the end of the second reading."

- Everyone: "Thanks be to God."

Note: If you wish, a pantomime of this scene could be performed while a narrator reads the text.

— Homily

"We are not blind like the men in the Gospel. We can see the sun... and the faces of those around us.

And yet, sometimes, it seems that it is our heart that is blind...

Our heart is blind when we don't see that those around us are in need of a smile, a favour, a pleasant "good morning", a "thank you"...

Our heart is blind when we refuse to admit our faults or to admit that others are right.

Our heart is blind when we refuse to understand that God asks us to be reconciled with each other.

Our heart is blind when we refuse to forget an unkind word or a mean gesture.

Let us ask God's forgiveness for the blindness of our hearts."

— Prayer

(Adapt this prayer along the lines of the conversations of the preceding days.)
- Responsory: "Forgive us, God our Father."

"Because we have forgotten or refused to pay attention to other people...

Because we are sometimes vengeful and because we do things that are unkind...

Because we don't sometimes have the courage to admit that we are wrong...

Because sometimes we wait too long before reconciling ourselves with others..."

Let us pray:
*"God our Father,
forgive me.
I have sinned against my brothers
and against you.
Cleanse me in your Spirit
so that I might grow in your love.
I ask this through Jesus our Lord. Amen."*
(Note: This prayer is taken from the child's booklet, p. 59.)

"Let us ask Jesus, who healed the eyes of the blind men, to heal our hearts with the light of his Spirit."

- Responsory: "Open our eyes, Lord."
"So that we are aware of those who are lonesome and who would like to play with us...

So that we realize when someone is tired and needs a helping hand...

So that we can simply admit that we are wrong...

So that we can discover people who need a smile or a kind word...

So that we can find the gesture or the words which will bring joy or courage to someone..."

- Leader:
"We know that God always forgives us. But he is asking us to make up for our sins, to seek together to grow in love.

Let us remain silent for a moment and ask the Lord Jesus to help us see how each one of us can bring more joy and happiness to our home, and to our family life."

(If the normal family atmosphere is conducive to this, these ideas could be shared by everyone. If not, continue on below.)

— **Rite**

The leader invites everyone in the family to show his desire to grow in love, by a sign of peace, for example: kissing each other, holding hands while singing a song, sharing some bread or cake...

If the celebration is before supper, the meal itself would be the sign of peace.

Through the following opening prayer, the family could become aware of the special significance of this meal:
"God our Father,
as we come together tonight for supper,
we want to tell you of our desire
to live more and more
in friendship and joy.

Help us to understand each other
and to forgive each other.

In a few days when we receive together
the sacrament of penance,
may we be cleansed by your Spirit
and strengthened in your love.

We ask this
through Jesus Christ your son
who is always with us. Amen."

When the sign of peace is merely a gesture, mention the sign of peace in the prayer instead of supper.

After supper or after the sign of peace, a song of friendship and joy could be sung together.

STAGE 6.
When we come back together again, there is great joy for all... we can achieve our project, God's Dream comes true again... and it is worth celebrating!

STAGE 6 The Church Invites Us to Celebrate God's Forgiveness

Summary

1. Number of Sessions

This stage is made up of three experiences:
- First session: The Prodigal Son
- Second session: The sacrament of penance
- Third session: Meditation preparing for the sacrament

2. General View of This Stage

With the sixth and final stage we come to the actual sacramental rite itself. There are three distinct parts to this stage:
— The first (p. 69) shows us in what spirit we should approach penance: in a spirit of celebration and rejoicing. The parable of the Prodigal Son is the core of this section.
— The second (p. 70-71), of a more practical nature, outlines what will be said between the child and the priest.
— Finally the third (p. 72-75) lets the child review the various aspects of his preparation on the evening before receiving the sacrament.

Please note that we do not go into detail concerning the ceremony. This is practically impossible, owing to the great diversity of opinion existing in the various parishes on this point. It is up to those immediately responsible (priest, parents or catechist) to decide on the necessary details.

3. Pedagogical Remarks

A. Try to avoid anything that could worry the child
The family atmosphere during this last stage is particularly important. If we seem worried and preoccupied about things of secondary importance, the child will be too...

This is why we should avoid any thoughts or attitudes that might risk concerning the child with:
- the anxiety of having to remember his sins,
- the details of the rites,
- a fear of the priest, or fear of God.

While talking to the child about the privacy of confession, assure him that the priest won't talk to anyone about the sins he confesses.

B. Approach the sacrament with joy and confidence
The whole spirit of this program should take the form of an invitation to celebrate together our joy in the Lord's forgiveness. In these final days it is important to experience fully this spirit with the child.

First Session: The Prodigal Son

Teaching Methods:
- *Using the booklet to start a conversation*
- *Narration or pantomime of the parable*
- *Drawing*

   1. *Using the booklet to start a conversation*
      - Read with the child pages 66 and 67.
        Point out the joy expressed in the pictures.
      - At this point it might be helpful to return to the first page of each stage in order to grasp the continuity of the program:
      p. 6: God loves us and invites us to share his life and happiness.
      p. 14: Each is different from others. We are important to God.
      p. 26: God invites us to help him in his Dream: e.g. to build a world of love.
      p. 38: We often answer his call. But we at times turn away from him and others.
      p. 50: God invites us to come back to him and also return to others.
      p. 66: It is a time of festival for God and for the Church when we celebrate the sacrament of peace. God's Dream comes true: love and happiness are reborn.

   2. *Narration or pantomime of the parable (p. 68-69)*
      — If you are alone with the child, tell the story of the parable, using the child's book.

      If this is a family session, the parable could be read aloud together, or told in pantomime form.

      — In the case of pantomiming, a narrator would read the text aloud and the father of the family would play the part of the Father. (It should be noted that when a scene from the Gospel is being pantomimed, it should be done in seriousness and with an atmosphere of faith.)

      — Commenting on the parable, emphasize:
         - the love of the Father who waited for his son to return and who forgave him everything:
         - the joy of the Father who wanted to celebrate his son's return by giving a huge feast.

   When the pantomime (or reading) is finished all could exchange impressions.
      — Then discuss the last paragraphs on page 69 which apply the parable to God our Father and to the sacrament of penance. Emphasize the following aspects:
         - God's mercy is infinite and far greater than any of the wrong things we can do.
         - It is Jesus' attitude toward sinners that helps us to understand this love of God.
         - In the sacrament of penance, the priest is there as a sign of the love of God who always forgives us.

3. *Making a drawing of the parable*
   Suggest that the child make a drawing about the parable — mention that in his drawing he should try to show the love of the father who is waiting for his son, and his joy when the son comes back.

   Underneath have him write this sentence:
   "It is a joy for God our Father to forgive his children."

Second Session: The Sacrament of Penance

Teaching Methods:
- A moment of reflection on the three pictures of the sacraments
- A conversation about the sacrament of penance

   1. *A moment of reflection on the three pictures of the sacraments*
      Before going into an explanation of the rites of the sacrament of penance, it would be good to help the child remember the other sacraments which he has received or will receive during his early years: baptism, confirmation, the eucharist.

      Here is a suggestion of how to do this:
      - Show the child the pictures in the Parents' Guide. Ask him what they mean. Let him talk about these three sacraments.

      - Read and discuss with the child the texts that accompany the pictures.

      "By the sign of baptism
      Jesus gives us a new life,
      the eternal life of God's children."

"By the sign of confirmation
Jesus gives us his Spirit
which will always be with us."

"By the sign of the eucharist
Jesus gives us himself
so that we can live united in love
with the Father and with all our brothers."

2. *A conversation about the sacrament of penance*

   A. *Talk about the sacrament of penance using the following as a guide:*

   - "We know that God always forgives us when we open our hearts to him. However he wants to give us a special sign of his forgiveness. Through the words of the priest, he wants us to hear his words of peace and forgiveness.

     By the sign of penance
     Jesus gives us God's forgiveness
     and the strength of the Holy Spirit, to help us become better."

   - "When we celebrate together with other Christians the sacrament of penance:
     — we confess together that we have sinned;
     — we ask God's forgiveness;
     — we celebrate our joy in being reconciled to God and to other people.
     Thus, the more united we are with each other, the more we can help each other grow in love."

   B. *Read and discuss with the child pages 70 and 71:*
      — Make the child aware of:
         - the actual details of the ceremony;
         - what he will say and do.
      Always bear in mind the customs of the parish.

      Try to avoid preoccupying him with secondary matters. Don't insist that he confess all his sins. That is only important in the case of mortal sins, which will not be discussed until much later with the child (see Stage 4, pedagogical remark B).

      What is important in his first few confessions is that he talk about the things he feels he did wrong.

      — Explain the meaning of the penance (or atonement) which he will be given by the priest: "It is the first step on the new road we are taking, it is a sign of our desire to turn again to God and to grow in love."

      The penance can take various forms: personal prayer, communal prayer, some gesture showing that we are sorry, etc. This should be discussed with the child in the light of the parent meetings.

      This discussion could be concluded with the prayer on page 67 or any other suitable prayer.

Third Session: Meditation in Preparation For the Sacrament

There are two possibilities:

A. THE CHILD COULD PREPARE HIMSELF WITH THE HELP OF ONE OR BOTH OF HIS PARENTS.

B. THE WHOLE FAMILY COULD TAKE PART IN A PREPARATORY VIGIL.

A. Individual Preparation

Remarks

— Personal preparation might be better for a child who is shy or worried. This preparation should preferably take place in the child's room just before bedtime.

— If the other children in the family so desire, they could also use the child's booklet to prepare themselves.

— Follow the suggestions given on pages 72 to 75 in the child's booklet.
- Together read slowly each paragraph.
- Take a few moments for silent reflection.
- Share together.
- Pray together.

— If the child seems unduly worried that he might forget what he wants to say to the priest, suggest that he write a few things down on a piece of paper and put it in one of the pockets of the clothes he will wear the next day. Normally however, at the age of 9 to 12 this should not be necessary.

— When saying goodnight to the child, be careful not to burden him with any material preoccupations concerning the following day, but rather try to leave him with a sense of peace and joy.

B. Family preparation

— Go through the pages of the booklet adapting them where necessary.

— The vigil should take place in an atmosphere of simplicity, reflection and peace.

— During the reflection period, some background music could be played.

After returning home

1. *Celebrate the event*
   After the celebration of penance, it would be good to honour the occasion with a small, intimate party, a special meal followed by:
   - a family outing

   OR
   - one of the children's favorite games.

   Try to avoid activities which might get the children too excited or cause any arguments.

   At the beginning of the meal, or as the evening prayer, pages 76 and 77 could be read, ending with a song of joy and praise.

2. *Speak of confessions to come*
   In the days that follow, talk to the child about the future, reading and discussing with him page 78: "When are you going to celebrate the sacrament of penance again?"

3. *Suggest to him the future use of his booklet*

   — Explain to the child that whenever he wishes to celebrate the sacrament of penance, he needs only take his book as a tool to pray and to think.

   — While going through the book with him, let him see that he may also use it at night to pray as he likes.

   — If other members of the family have participated in the program, the book could be left in a place where it is available to all.

PART FIVE

Suggestions for Family Life and Prayer

To the extent that the family has participated in the program and has enjoyed it, they might wish to continue along the same line and to renew certain prayer sessions and group discussions.

Part Five was designed to meet this need. In it can be found:

- Family rites at meal time
- Family rites during evening prayer
- Family discussions and celebrations.

Nature and Advantages of These Family Rites

As we have already stated, christian reconciliation is experienced directly in the day-to-day events of our lives, while it is celebrated "officially", as it were, in the sacrament.

But between these two extremes, there is a place for simple family rites that form part of the whole texture of our lives.

    A. *The nature of these rites*
    Essentially these are
- gestures of peace and friendship,
- experienced in God's presence,
- and made verbally explicit through prayer.

    The tone of these rites can be different. There can be a simple expression of a desire for reconciliation, or of a feeling of joy in being together.

    The greater the role played by the family in the creation of these gestures — depending on its own character, its particular spiritual experiences, and the circumstances at that time — the more significant and authentic the rites will be.

    B. *The advantages of these rites*

    Among the many advantages we will signal out two:

- The first is that it keeps the family "alert" to God's call, and humbly aware of its sinfulness.

    If we regularly experience together this type of prayer, assuming, of course, that it is meaningful to us, then it becomes difficult to remain mediocre and self-satisfied.

- The second advantage lies in having a chance to let the little tensions, edginess, etc. which inevitably result from life together, melt away. We cannot always be asking for forgiveness. And yet there are always small areas of friction which are not big enough to ask forgiveness for, but which create a certain uneasiness. A family rite of reconciliation helps relax the situation, while emphasizing the deep-seated wish of everyone to reconcile differences and to be reunited.

    For example:
    A family had the custom of saying grace while holding hands, at one of the Saturday meals when everyone was there. This was a way of saying to one another before the Sunday Eucharist: "Forgive me for being unkind, I love you just the same!"

I — Family Rites at Meals

The examples given here are ones which different families have experienced.

Example 1: Coming together

— Gesture: The family stands together around the table.

— Prayer: The father or the mother prays aloud:

> "God our Father,
> look at us here, your children
> gathered together in your presence,
> around this table.
>
> Let your Spirit come upon us,
> so that we may become more aware
> of the needs of one another.
>
> We ask this
> through Jesus Christ your son
> who gave his life for us. Amen"

Note: The middle verse can be varied as follows:
> so that we may be more patient
> toward one another
>   or
> so that we can learn to forgive
> one another.

Example 2: The offering and breaking of bread
If one of the parents or children could bake some bread for a special occasion, this could be the basis for the following suggestion:

— Gesture: The one who cooked the bread holds it in his hands during the prayer. It is shared with all after the prayer.

— Prayer: "God our Father,
> we offer you this bread
> that X... has made for us.
>
> Let it become for you
> a sign of our desire
> to live more and more
> united in love
> as your Son Jesus
> showed us. Amen."

The father or the mother brings out the meaning of the sharing:
"When we share this bread
let each one of us think in his heart,
how we can better share our life,
our talents, our time
with one another."

Sharing:
Divide the bread into small pieces.
Pass the basket of bread to each person.
Wait until everyone has a piece.
Eat the bread together in silence.

Song: Finish with a short song of joy and friendship.

Note: This rite could be varied by using, at the end of the meal, a cake prepared by someone in the family.

Example 3: Offering and sharing of wine
The glasses should be filled and put on a tray.
If the youngest children do not drink wine, they could be given fruit juice.
This rite is particularly appropriate for special occasions.

— Gesture: One of the parents holds the tray of glasses during the offering prayer.

— Prayer: "God our Father,
we offer you this wine which we are going to share.
Let it be a sign of our joy,
the joy of living in your presence,
the joy of living together united in love.

Let the Holy Spirit come into our hearts,
so that he can teach us to share our joy,
with those who are lonesome and unhappy,
and to whom you send us.

We ask this through Jesus Christ your Son. Amen."

— Gesture: The wine is joyfully shared.

— Song of joy.

Remark: During the meal the conversation could be about those to whom God is sending us to share our joy, and about what can be done for them...

II — Family Rites During Evening Prayer

This kind of rite will be more of an "examination of conscience". Only the outline is given here; variations can be made on this.

- a) Remember God's call

    The person who is directing the prayer should remind the family of God's call by using a short biblical text adapted to the circumstances and by introducing it with a few words.

- b) Examining ourselves in the light of this call

    This is a true examination of conscience. It can be done in many ways. We suggest two:

    — Let each person meditate in silence.

    — Help direct their meditation by using several simple questions. It is important that these questions be applicable to the life of the adults as well as the children.
- c) Ask for God's forgiveness

    The following can be used here:

    — a prayer of contrition which everyone likes or which everyone makes up together (the child's booklet has several);

    — a litany prayer like the one suggested in the celebration in Stage 5, third session

    Remark: In cases where an incident worthy of note has occurred during the day either between the two parents, or the children with each other, or the children and their parents, those responsible could, if they wished, show that they are sorry either in words, or by some silent gesture.

    But this should happen only occasionally and never be forced. Obviously it is up to the parents to set the tone. They should not be afraid that this act of humility will lessen their children's respect for them. Rather the opposite will happen: the children will be very sensitive to the truthful attitude taken by the adults.

- d) Ask the help of the Holy Spirit

    It would then be good to ask the Holy Spirit for his help in seeing how to "grow in love" and in doing what is necessary to achieve this. All could be invited to meditate for a few moments in silence.

e) End with a prayer of confidence

Choose or compose a closing prayer which expresses our confidence in the Lord. Then depending on the circumstances, we could sing a song of praise to the Virgin Mary or some other song.

Important remarks concerning these rites of peace:

How frequently should these rites be practised? It is up to each family to decide this, depending on its life-style and its internal relationships.

In general it can be said:

- If the family wishes to make these rites a regular part of their christian life, then they should decide together from experience what is best for them.

  Making it a weekly thing seems to be best for many families. There is an added advantage of having it the day before the celebration of the Eucharist, and using it as preparation for this.

  Care should be taken that these rites don't become routine through too frequent use. Having them every day would certainly be too much.

- When there are some outstanding difficulties in the life of the family, a rite of peace could be experienced together in order to reestablish an atmosphere of good feeling, or to celebrate it if it has already been reestablished.

- Certain special occasions — an anniversary, a special visitor — could be a good time for a rite of peace expressing the joy of living together.

III — Family Discussions and Celebrations

If everyone enjoyed the family discussions and celebrations suggested in the program, they might want to continue with this experience and to integrate these two events in the family's activities.

Here are some suggestions for this:

A. *Family discussions*
The goal of family discussion is to help the family "take stock of themselves", "see themselves in the light of the Gospel." These discussions can be oriented toward two objectives:
- the attitudes and responsibilities of the family group toward the outside world;
- the quality of christian life experienced internally by the family.

a) Family responsibilities

For these types of discussions there are suggestions in the Guide (cf. p. 119)

These discussions should not take place too frequently.
They should be used when the circumstances warrant, or at certain key moments in the year, for example:

- when the family is deciding at the beginning of the year what part they will play in the life of the neighbourhood, or when they are evaluating their actions at the end of the year;

- or again when the family is planning their vacations and they try to decide together if their responsibility as a family, towards other people or groups of other people, should be considered in their plans.

b) Internal life of the family

The other type of family discussion tries to center on the quality of christian life experienced internally by the family.

For example, efforts at discussion can be made concerning the prayer life of the family, the quality of relationships, mutual aid and each person's responsibilities in the family.

(In order to organize these discussions, refer to page 130 in this guide.)

The circumstances of life and the great liturgical events of the year will serve as inspiration in choosing the most opportune moments for this type of communal reflection.

Remark: With these two types of discussion, it would be good to remember the following two principles when deciding the times, themes and conditions of these discussions:

— *Be guided by the basic needs of the family, and by the demands of the moment.*

— *Try to do everything as naturally as possible, in an atmosphere of mutual confidence, joint decisions and faith.*

B. Family celebrations

The organization of family celebrations should also take into account the two principles just mentioned.

The important thing is that the family prays together whenever it feels a need. Here again, this should not be something that is imposed, but everything should be decided together.

Three or four times a year, in order to make a particular family or liturgical event more special, the family could experience together a rather long, really elaborate celebration. Time should then be taken to prepare it thouroughly in advance.

But generally, in the course of the year, what is really needed is some time to experience moments of special prayer. The suggested rites of peace during a meal or the evening prayer, could be a further source of ideas in this area.

The more the entire family takes part in preparing these times of prayer, the better they will be.

Three elements are basic to these times of prayer:
- Life, with all its questions, joys and pain.
- The living word of God which summons us to seek life's inmost source of enlightenment and final meaning.
- Heartfelt prayer inspired by the Holy Spirit, which may be either an expression of praise or a call for help, depending on the circumstances and which gives greater unity to family life.

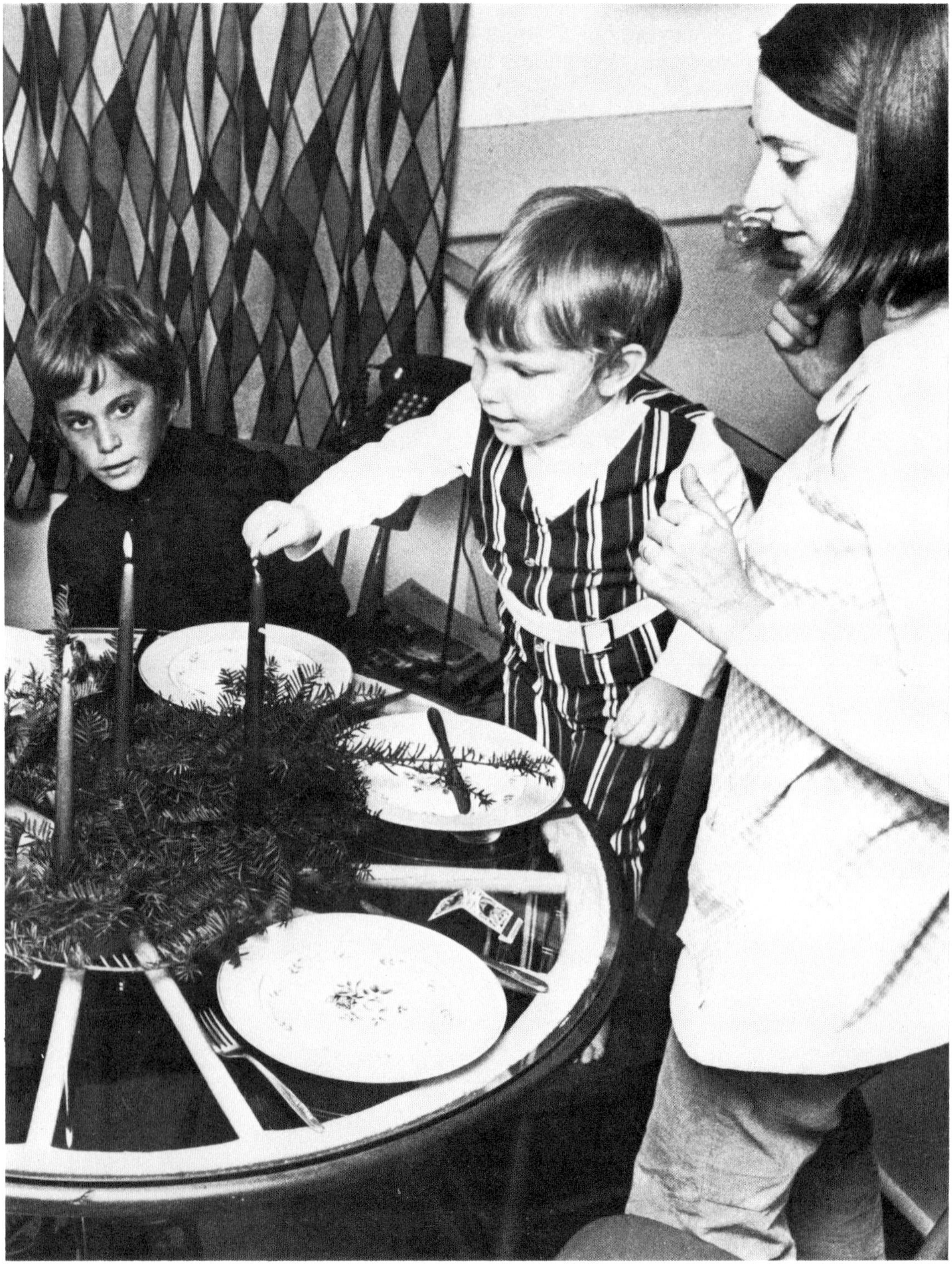

In short...

QUESTIONS THAT BOTHER PARENTS

1. **Should mortal sin be discussed?**
   This does not seem necessary before the first few confessions.

   A little later it could be discussed along the following lines:
   - "If you have a fight with one of your friends and if you do something very mean to him on purpose, your friendship with him is destroyed, it is as if it were dead; it can only come alive again if you go to him and you clearly show that you are sorry."

   - "When we turn away from God, when we do something on purpose that is seriously wrong, we destroy our friendship with him, and it is as if it were dead. This is what is known as mortal sin."

   - "Even when this happens God continues to love us, he is ready to forgive us. He invites us to come to him in the sacrament of penance."

   - "If we are guilty of a mortal sin, the Church asks that we go to confession before taking part in the celebration of the Eucharist. She asks that we do this as a sign that we are truly sorry for what we have done, that we really want to turn to God again."

   For more information, see Parents Guide, p.124 .

2. **Should the child be given a list of sins to help him in his examination of conscience?**

   Even though this may seem at first to be the easiest way, there are several serious defects in this method, among them, the risk of keeping the child locked in his childish view of morality, based on what is permitted and what is forbidden.

   For more details concerning this question, read pages 124-125 of the Parents' Guide.

3. **How can we help a child examine his conscience?**

   Essentially
   - by making the child aware of God's invitation to him, expressed, for instance, in some of Jesus' own words;

   - by encouraging him to think about his life in order to discover how he has answered God's call.

   For more information see:

   Child's Book (7-8): p. 18-19 and 41-42.
   Child's Book (9 to 12): p. 36-37; 42-43 and 74.

4. **Should he be given a list of the ten commandments before making his first confession?**

   - If the child already knows them, he could simply be shown how these commandments help us understand God's call to love Him and to love other people.

   - If the child does not already know them, it would be preferable to tell him about them in the weeks following his first confession rather than burdening him with them now.

   - In any case, all the parts of the ten commandments that apply to a child are presented to him in a different form in his booklet.

5. **Should he memorize an act of contrition? If so, which one?**

   - Yes, it would be good for a child to know an act of contrition by heart.

   - However, the traditional ones are little suited to his age.

   - If there is no particular act of contrition which the diocese or parish insists on using, you could
     — make one up with the child,
     — help him learn one of the prayers of contrition suggested in his booklet.

6. **Should the child learn a set formula for confession?**

    - If this is demanded by the parish, obviously you must conform to the customs of the parish.

    - If nothing is specifically required, it would be better to explain to him clearly what he should say and do, but without imposing a special set of words on him.

7. **When should we first begin to discuss sin with the child?**

    You should avoid talking about it too soon, as you risk distorting the child's image of God. Sin should not be discussed with the child until after you have taken a long time to awaken in the child, the sense of joy that comes with the knowledge that God loves us.
    See: Parents' Guide, p.26 -

8. **When should the moral formation of a child begin?**

   The moral formation of a child should begin very early, as he experiences different kinds of joy in his interpersonal relationships.

   This formation should be a discovery of fundamental human values.
   It should not be linked too soon to a child's religious formation.
   See: Parents' Guide, p. 19-23.

9. **How often should a child go to confession?**

   The child should feel free:
   - he should go to confession any time he wants to;
   - he should never be forced to go to confession.

   However it would be good to remind him at certain times, (for example the major events of the liturgical calendar: Advent, Easter, etc.), that the Church encourages Christians to celebrate the sacrament of penance together.

   The best way to do this is obviously to suggest that the child accompany you when you are going to celebrate this sacrament.
   See: Child's Book (9 to 12): p. 78 and 79.

10. **Should we celebrate a child's first confession?**

    Yes certainly, but make sure that this celebration is carried out with characteristic simplicity and intimacy. The child need not be given secular gifts. He himself is not the cause for celebration, rather it is the joy he experiences in his encounter with God. This is the best present!

Nihil Obstat:
Rev. Jacques Fournier
Montreal, November 3, 1973

Imprimatur:
Most Reverend Leonard J. Crowley, D.D.
Montreal, November 28, 1973

Photo Credits:

Photographic Research: Kovitek Ltd.
Robert Chiasson: cover photo, pp. 10, 20, 97
Normand Cadorette: pp. 35, 50
Ellefsen: p. 9
Jean-Marie Faber: pp. 7, 8, 16, 44, 53, 56, 91, 154
J. Krieber: p. 2
Serge Laurin: p. 31

Published by Paulist Press
Editorial Office: 1865 Broadway. N.Y., N.Y. 10023
Business Office: 400 Sette Drive, Paramus, N.J. 07652